Christian Bjørnskov

Happiness

in the Nordic World

Aarhus University Press / The University of Wisconsin Press

The Nordic World
Happiness in the Nordic World
© Christian Bjørnskov 2021

Cover, layout, and typesetting:
Camilla Jørgensen, Trefold
Cover photograph: Poul Ib Henriksen
Figures: Christian Bjørnskov
Copy editors: Heidi Flegal and Mia Gaudern
Acquisitions editors: Amber Rose Cederström
and Karina Bell Ottosen
This book is typeset in FS Ostro and printed
on Munken Lynx 130 g
Printed by Narayana Press, Denmark
Printed in Denmark 2021

ISBN 978 87 7219 325 0
ISBN 978 0 299 33404 8

This book is available in a digital edition

Library of Congress Cataloging-in-Publication
data is available

Published with the generous support of the
Aarhus University Research Foundation,
the Carlsberg Foundation, and the Nordic
Council of Ministers

The Nordic World series is copublished by
Aarhus University Press and the University
of Wisconsin Press

Aarhus University Press
aarhusuniversitypress.dk

The University of Wisconsin Press
uwpress.wisc.edu

PEER
REVIEWED

MIX
Paper
FSC FSC® C010651

Contents

Chapter 1

Introduction

Of all the regions in the world, the Nordic region – Denmark, Finland, Iceland, Norway, and Sweden – turns out to be the happiest, based on people's responses when asked how happy they are. At first this fact seems improbable: The United States is much richer, Portugal has much nicer weather, and it was the French who invented the concept of *joie de vivre* – the joy of living. So how can a region that is situated on the periphery of the inhabited world, which is ice-cold and uncomfortably dark all winter, be one of the nicest places to live? That is the question this book seeks to answer. Throughout its chapters, I will use that question to explore what thirty years of happiness research can tell us, thereby also shedding light on how the Nordics are special.

The starting point of the book is that everyone wants to live a good life. We may have very different definitions of exactly what "a good life" is, and our conceptions of what it ought to be may be utterly wrong. From the Buddhist monk meditating on life, or the gifted high-school student contemplating her career ambitions, to the racing driver dreaming about the perfect lap at Le Mans, the search for fulfillment is common to virtually all human beings. The "pursuit of happiness" is not only written into the US

Declaration of Independence, it is also the main theme of countless books, plays, and songs. Shakespeare's Romeo yearns for his Juliet; Mark Twain's Huckleberry Finn seeks adventure on the Mississippi river; and Chekhov's Uncle Vanya strives for happiness, but makes his own life impossible.

Philosophers have spent more than two thousand years pondering this question, and particularly thinking about what "the good life" ought to be. Ever since Socrates, Plato, and Aristotle strolled around ancient Athens, and Seneca advised the Roman emperor Nero, most philosophers and social thinkers have, at some point in their careers, thought deeply about what people should do to live a good, happy life – and whether, indeed, anyone can know what other people ought to do. Their attempts have produced great theories and insights, but have also given rise to a veritable flood of self-help books. Yet this book is emphatically *not* about the philosophy of happiness – so it is *not* about how other people believe we ought to lead our lives to make the most of them.

Instead, it is about why some people are happier than others, and particularly why the inhabitants of the Nordic countries, on average, are happier than almost anyone else in the world. Throughout the book, the answers given to these questions rest on recent research in a field of scientific inquiry that has become known as "happiness studies." This field is multidisciplinary, and scholars from anthropology, psychology, sociology, economics, and political science all contribute regularly to its development. The field even has its own prestigious journal – the *Journal of Happiness Studies* – where researchers share their new findings. Its multidisciplinarity is so palpable that it is often impossible to tell whether an article was written by a psychologist, an economist, or a political scientist, because they share the same questions, the same survey data, and often even the same methods. In the fol-

8

lowing, therefore, I ignore the boundaries between these fields and simply cover insights from happiness studies. These insights provide a number of pieces to the puzzle of why some people are happier than others, and why the Nordic peoples are the happiest of all.

The purpose of this book first requires us to define what we are talking about, and to address the problem that most languages use one word – being "happy" – to describe two quite different phenomena. Making this distinction also involves knowing how happiness can be measured, and in which parts of the world people are happiest. Throughout the rest of the book, I will use the data and measures from large international surveys, described in detail later, to illustrate what makes people happy – and what, surprisingly, does not – as well as how the Nordics differ from the rest of the world. In other words, the book rests on the *empirical* literature on happiness that is based on people's answers to questions about happiness and life satisfaction.

However, before moving on to the many insights I can share about the elusively happy Nordics, I need to divulge the first big surprise in happiness research: Even though people live under extremely different conditions in more than 200 countries and on continents that are far apart, they are all still human beings, which makes them surprisingly similar. The same fundamental factors are important to the happiness of a couple of about the same age in Ghana, Denmark, and Peru. As you read the rest of this book, please keep this in mind: People have very different tastes and norms, but they still share the same basic hopes, needs, and aspirations, no matter where they live.

Before I move on to confirming some of the existing "folk theory" – the commonly held beliefs about what ought to make people happy – and destroying other strongly held beliefs about what "the good life" is, it is important to ask readers to let go of their own folk theory and keep an open mind throughout the book. People who plan their lives based on such sayings may be doing themselves a great disservice. To know what is up and down in these discussions, we first need to know what we are talking about. The next chapter therefore deals with what happiness is, and what we are measuring. Subsequent chapters explore what we know about the effects of a number of different things on how happy and satisfied people are: the big things in life, such as marriage, children, age, and one's job, income, and wealth, as well as trust and institutions, and freedom and tolerance.

Throughout the book, I compare international survey evidence from the Nordic countries – Denmark, Finland, Iceland, Norway, and Sweden – with three other regions of the world: the rest of what is commonly known as the Western world, the formerly communist countries of Central and Eastern Europe, and Latin America. While the book tells the broader story of why some people are happier than others, these comparisons serve to highlight how, and how much, the Nordics actually differ from the rest of the world. With all this in mind, the last chapter summarizes how, despite all the human commonalities, the Nordics are, nevertheless, a region that stands out.

Chapter 2.

What is happiness?

It is easy to get the impression that there are many profound maxims about happiness and how to become happy. Mark Twain is sometimes credited with saying that "Sanity and happiness are an impossible combination." Similarly, a Danish film evergreen from 1937, still played and sung today, asks why happiness is so fickle, and why joy doesn't last – although most of the proverbs, sayings, and self-help slogans around the world convey a more positive message. However, the question much of the scientific happiness literature really asks is this: Do these proverbs and sayings reveal people's experiences, or do they reflect what people think ought to have made them happy?

The proverbs express what is often called "folk theory," which is made up of people's shared beliefs and ideas about what makes "the good life." Many people say, for example, that money *won't* make you happy, but as we shall see in Chapter 4, which is about income, this is actually not true. Folk theory also says that children, peace and quiet, respect for traditions, and not wanting too much will contribute to a person's happiness, and it also emphasizes family and friendship. Much of the recent self-help literature tries to make people feel satisfied with what they already have, and focus on some balance or other in their lives. In certain places in the world, the idea of a harmonious balance between different elements is important in people's norms and conceptions of the good life. Harmony, for example, plays a major role in Asian philosophies of the good or virtuous life, and a Finnish proverb says that "happiness is a place between too little and too much." The versatile Swedish word *lagom* – which is an adverb, an adjective, and a noun – even expresses this blissful point between too much and too little: *Lagom* is when something is like the perfect porridge in the fairytale of Goldilocks and the Three Bears, which was *just* the right temperature.

The word *lagom* has been used to explain why the Nordics are so happy – because people strike just the right balance – but it is worth noting that neither the expression nor the word has a counterpart in Danish, Icelandic, or Norwegian. Similarly, both folk theory and social norms about what is "socially acceptable" in life vary across different cultures and countries. They can also change dramatically over time, as the example of gender norms shows: Very few Europeans today would accept the norms that constrained women's life decisions in the 1930s, just as very few Europeans would personally accept the religious norms of contemporary Iran, or the strict family structures in parts of Africa. As such, many of our norms, traditions, and even long-held conceptions of what the good life ought to be can be powerfully misleading.

The two types of happiness

One of the main challenges is that in virtually all languages, people use the word "happy" to describe two quite different phenomena: immediate sensations of great joy and contentment, and a broader and long-lasting state of satisfaction and well-being in daily life. We say that we are happy when we experience a brief burst of great joy, and we may also say that we have a happy life, but for quite different reasons. One of these concepts is a short-lived phenomenon, while the other is a more thoroughly considered long-run assessment of how we experience our lives in the broader perspective.

Brief bursts of happiness can be caused by many things. Imagine a Christmas gift you have been dreaming of all December, or remember that special moment your beloved said "Yes!" when you proposed, or the day your first child was born, or the Sunday the New England Patriots won the Superbowl. Most of us experience such moments and remember them vividly; they are the short-lived version of happiness, or what many psychologists prefer to call "positive affect" (Kuppens, Realo, & Diener 2008). This is the feeling of your brain rewarding you for behavior that is either good for you personally or good for the survival of the human species. Conversely, we all know what the reverse feels like – when your home team loses a crucial qualifying match (again) or when you just miss the last train home, not to mention the seemingly endless limbo in an airport when your flight has been cancelled. Psychologists often prefer to call such experiences "negative affect" to separate them from more lasting feelings of misery, as in the case of grief or depression, for example.

"Positive affect" describes the experiences of happiness we often refer to as "fickle" – inconstant and unpredictable – but fortunately, the same applies to their reverse. We have several expressions for this sort of happiness, and its opposite, which one often sees in the literature. "Positive affect" is only one expression; "euphoria" and "dopamine happiness" are also in common use, because dopamine and other similar neurotransmitters are released in the human brain's reward center, known as the *nucleus accumbens*, in such situations. This center functions like a dog that wags its tail when it is happy: It is jubilant when we do something it perceives as good, but it becomes despondent when we do something it perceives as bad. Dopamine happiness, positive affect, or euphoric emotions are what we sometimes see manifested very clearly in teenagers. Their affect can rapidly shift from positive to negative, their mood changing dramatically. A teenager can feel miserable at breakfast, joyful at lunch, and utterly indifferent at the dinner table.

The other type of happiness is very different from the brief ups and downs in positive and negative affect. To investigate it, researchers look at how happy we are between life's mental Kodak moments: How happy are we in our daily lives? This is often referred to as "everyday happiness," "wedded bliss," or "bread-and-butter happiness" by popular journalists and lifestyle writers. Researchers in the field instead prefer to call it "subjective well-being" when exploring how people perceive their lives as a whole.

Although the neurobiological foundation of subjective well-being is far less developed than our understanding of affect, people's long-run assessments of their lives are known to be associated with a center in the brain called the prefrontal cortex. The *nucleus accumbens*, which is associated with affect or short-lived happiness, is a very old part of the brain in evolutionary terms. The prefrontal cortex, on the other hand, is a relatively young part of the brain; very few animals show development in this area, besides human beings. Long-term happiness is, in other words, fundamentally different from short-lived affect.

In this book, I therefore draw a sharp distinction between these two phenomena, as the general meaning of "being happy" during events or moments that make us intensely happy and the broader feeling that "our life as a whole is a happy one" are completely different. We risk deceiving ourselves when using a single word – "happy" – to describe these two distinct phenomena. I would also like to emphasize that the focus in the rest of the book is on the long-term variety of happiness – our subjective well-being.

How to measure happiness

Researchers, including Ruut Veenhoven, Carol Graham, and myself, have tried different approaches when seeking to measure happiness, but have come to the consensus that the best approach is to ask people directly. However, we do so with a twist: While we normally prefer to define the terms we use before starting any study, happiness studies are different in that they do *not* define any terms before putting questions to participants. Instead, the approach is to ask people directly how happy they are in general. This allows them to answer the questions based on their own definition of happiness, their own preferences, and their own situation in life. If we defined the term "happiness" before asking people, their answers would be based on how close they felt they were to our definition of happiness, and not to their own. Of course, some researchers still prefer to use objective measures, in which they themselves or other social scientists have defined what happiness ought to be. There is nothing wrong with that kind of research, but it cannot tell us much about what ordinary people actually value in their lives.

Another challenge when asking people about their lives – and when communicating modern happiness research – is the word "happy." In most Nordic languages (with the exception of Finnish), the word for happiness is *lykke*, and being happy is being *lykkelig*.[1] The word is obviously related to the English word "luck" and the German *Glück*, which means both happiness and luck or fortune. Language can be deceptive, which foreigners living in the Nordic countries quickly learn, as with the Danish word for "an accident," *en ulykke*, which literally means "an unhappiness." They also learn that to translate the English "happy," the Nordic languages offer two options, the stronger of which are *lykkelig*-type words, so being *lykkelig* is a bigger deal than just being happy.

1.
These Danish words have close equivalents in Norwegian and Swedish. In Finland, the word for "happy" is *onnelinen*, and in Estonia (which has linguistic ties to Finland and cultural similarities to the Nordics) it is *õnnelik*

The problems of conveying the concept of "happiness" can be avoided by asking people how satisfied they are with their lives as a whole. The word "satisfied" turns out to be much easier to translate precisely than the word "happy." Furthermore, in and outside the Nordic countries, where both questions have been asked, the distributions of the responses match up: Very few people answer the two questions differently, so those who are happy are also satisfied, and those who are not are dissatisfied with their lives. In international comparisons, most researchers in happiness studies therefore prefer to use questions such as "How satisfied are you with your life as a whole these days?"[2]

Some version of this question has been included in a growing number of surveys around the world since the mid-1970s. It is included in several national surveys, such as the US General Social Survey and the British Social Attitudes Survey. Internationally, some sort of life satisfaction question is also included in the various barometer surveys – the EuroBarometer, Latinobarometer, Afrobarometer, Asian and East Asian barometers, and the Arab Barometer – as well as the European Social Survey, the Latin American Public Opinion Project surveys, and the gigantic Gallup World Poll.[3] However, it remains an open question just how comparable the slightly different questions from these surveys are.

Throughout this book, I therefore use data from a large international questionnaire survey called the World Values Survey (WVS) and its European counterpart, the European Values Study (EVS). The WVS was first conducted in 1980-1982 in a small number of countries and has since been repeated and expanded across the world. I use the most recent version of the WVS, known as "the seventh wave," which covered 77 countries spread across the world in 2017-2020 and included the EVS conducted in 2017. It asks the question "How satisfied are you with

2.
A few scholars instead use "experience sampling," as in Nobel laureate Daniel Kahnemann's "Day Reconstruction Method," which asks respondents to reconstruct their day and assess how they felt during different activities. This method shows interesting patterns, but it cannot tell us whether a person's experiences during the day affect their long-term happiness

3.
These surveys, with the exception of the Gallup World Poll, are available free of charge. Used for thousands of scientific papers, they are also suitable for ordinary readers with basic statistical literacy

your life as a whole these days?" and gives respondents a choice ranging from 1 (Dissatisfied) to 10 (Satisfied). However, to emphasize certain important aspects, I sometimes supplement the WVS data with information from other surveys.

Happiness in different populations

The WVS data suggest that there are large differences across the world. As Figure 2.1 shows, the four regions that we will focus on in this book have quite different satisfaction averages: People in the Nordics on average rate their life satisfaction at 7.97; people in Western countries outside of the Nordics rate theirs at 7.27; people in Latin America rate their life satisfaction at 7.76; and those in the formerly communist countries of Central and Eastern Europe at 7.09. However, Figure 2.1 also includes the average life satisfaction per region from the Gallup World Poll (GWP). While the averages are slightly smaller, as the GWP uses a so-called Cantril ladder and a scale from 0 to 10, these differences are also much larger than in the WVS: The average in the Nordics is 7.55; in the rest of the West, 6.58; in Latin America, 6.16; and 5.57 in formerly communist countries.

Figure 2.1 Average life satisfaction, four regions

Average life satisfaction

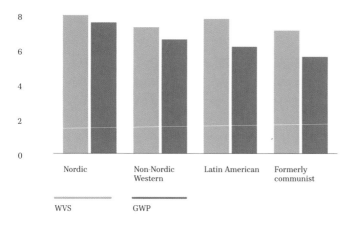

WVS   GWP

As the figure illustrates, whether one uses one method or the other, the Nordic region emerges as the happiest in the world, although the implication is that one should never draw conclusions based on a single survey. Surveys are never as precise as one might hope, and random events can also affect how people respond to surveys.[4] While Iraq consistently appears as one of the least satisfied places in the world, with scores in the WVS and GWP of 4.5 and 4.4, respectively, survey results in other countries appear inconsistent. Average life satisfaction of Zimbabweans in the WVS is 4.9, while it is only 3.7 in the GWP, though this difference may be a result of one of the surveys being conducted very soon after the military coup in November 2017. Conversely, it is difficult to reconcile the results of the two surveys in Myanmar, where the WVS shows a very high level of satisfaction of 7.2, whereas the GWP shows a very low level of only 4.4. The example from Myanmar should remind us that in some less democratic countries, it can be difficult to conduct surveys without government intervention and attempts to control the outcome. Not all

4.
See Hariri, Bjørnskov, & Justesen (2016) for findings on how an unforeseen currency devaluation in Botswana in 2011 significantly reduced life satisfaction. It was announced while the AfroBarometer survey in Botswana was ongoing, so some respondents were surveyed just days before the devaluation, and others up to two weeks after. This enabled us to compare the two groups

autocracies "massage" their survey data – far from it – but some of them evidently have an interest in presenting their populations as happier than they really are.[5]

5.
Care is advisable when using survey data from China, Cuba, Iran, and Myanmar. Magee & Doces (2015) also recommends a cautious approach to other data, for example on budgets, from these countries

Figure 2.2 illustrates how significant the problem is. As the figure makes clear, the two surveys – the WVS and the GWP – exhibit very similar patterns across the rich Western countries (the olive dots). The two surveys also, in general, show quite similar results for formerly communist countries (the pink dots), although one can see how average life satisfaction in Albania, Bosnia and Herzegovina, and Croatia appears much higher in the WVS than in the GWP. Conversely, there is practically no agreement between the WVS and GWP measures across the 11 Latin American countries covered by both surveys.

The frankly peculiar picture in Figure 2.2 illustrates one of the open questions in happiness research that this book does not – and cannot – answer. Among researchers in the field, it is known as "the Latin American problem": Why are most Latin American countries so much happier than outsiders might think, and why do the differences within Latin America often appear so erratic and unsystematic? Fortunately, the differences among people and countries across the rest of the world are systematic and predictable in ways that have given us many insights over the last three decades into what makes people happy, and particularly into how the Nordic countries are different. These are the insights we will discuss in the rest of the book.

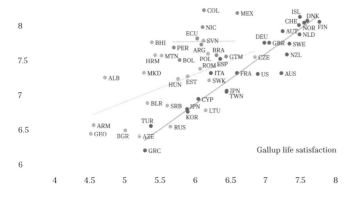

Figure 2.2 World Values Survey versus Gallup World Poll

Chapter 3.

The big things in life

The first question is whether "the big things in life" – finding the right partner, getting married, having and enjoying good social relations, family, and friends, having and raising children, finding a job, and having a normal working life, as well as one's age and life situation – really affect how people perceive their lives. In other words, do the things and people we care most about in our lives also make us happier? And are people in the Nordic countries different from people in the rest of the world when it comes to what matters the most?

While it may sound trivial to say that social relations are one of the most important sources of happiness and satisfaction, this is confirmed by practically all studies in the happiness literature. In 2008, for instance, Nattavudh Powdthavee used a method that is common in economics to put a "price tag" on social interactions. Using British data, he found that a substantial improvement in social involvement gave the same increase in satisfaction as an income increase worth 85,000 pounds, or roughly 115,000 US dollars (Powdthavee 2008). Whether it is our family, our friends, our neighbors, our colleagues, or the many other people we meet, they contribute to our lives in many ways.

One of the main findings is that people with a committed life partner are substantially happier than people who are either single or recently divorced. Nevertheless, this topic is particularly difficult to deal with, because such a relationship is what is technically termed "endogenous": People become happier when they find "the one," but people who are already happier will probably find it easier to find a partner. After all, very few people are likely to be attracted by a gloomy, grumpy person. That individuals nonetheless become happier on finding someone to share their lives with is supported by the fact that they also become less happy after a divorce or a break-up.

Exploring the WVS data, we see that in Western countries outside the Nordics, people who are either married or in a stable relationship are about 5% (.38 points) happier than those who are not. Within the five Nordic countries, the difference between the two groups is even larger, at 10% (.77 points). However, if you follow the same people over time, as the British economist Andrew Clark has done, it turns out that happiness increases in the year before their wedding, then returns to normal in the year after their wedding.

As noted above, the additional happiness people experience when getting married is temporary, while the happiness they already had having met their "one and only" is permanent. The happiness people derive from a stable relationship can come from a multitude of channels: Having a partner means there is someone to talk to every day, who can share one's good and bad experiences, help bear one's burdens, ease one's pains, and perhaps also provide another perspective on many things in life. How, exactly, the benefits of having a partner arise is unknown, because there are so many ways in which it could have an influence.

Outside of the family, social relations and networks are also important contributors to happiness. The type of social relations one has, and the voluntary networks one engages in and enjoys, is a matter of personal preferences and interests. While one person may derive enjoyment and meaning from being engaged in a political party, and another may get the same enjoyment and happiness from singing in a choir or helping at the local church, my personal preference is playing at the tennis club and spending time with the other members. At any rate, spending time with other people and sharing a common interest appears to make everyone a lot happier, and the reasons are probably very similar to the reasons why having a committed partner makes everyone happier. As long as relationships and activities are voluntary, social relations are one of the most important determinants of happiness. And, as we shall see below, they are also one of the reasons why people with a job are substantially happier than those who are unemployed.

The value of social networks can be gauged using a simple example from the WVS, which asks people if they are active or inactive members of a range of different specified associations. These answers can also be used to solve one of the problems with establishing the importance of social relations: Are people with more social relations happier, or are happier people just more likely to have many social relations, because they are more pleasant people? The clever solution is to compare people who are not members of a specific association with people who are members, and to compare inactive members – who do not enjoy social relations in the association – with people who are active members. Comparing non-members with members in sports associations in the WVS shows that *active* members are about 4% (.3 points) more satisfied with their lives than people who are either not members or inactive. Even if many of the non-members may not like sports and are members of other associations, the additional satisfaction must therefore derive from being active and having social relations in the sports association.

The amount of socializing Nordic people do may be one of the reasons why their countries are rated the happiest in the world. From fisheries associations and agricultural cooperatives to philanthropic societies and sports clubs, the Nordic societies are suffused with voluntary associations. An old joke in Denmark goes that if two Danes meet, they have a chat and a cup of coffee. If three Danes meet, they set up an association. The majority of the Nordic populations are members of some form of association – quite often a soccer club or other sports club – and children are brought up with this type of densely social civil society.

According to some researchers, most famously the American political scientist Robert Putnam, these associations are often structurally different from associations and networks in other parts of the world. Like patrons in a British pub, the moment Nordic members step into their tennis club, arrive on the soccer pitch, or start choir practice, their objective social status, education, and wealth cease to matter.[6] Nordic civil society is typically characterized by diversity, thereby creating what Putnam calls "bridging social capital" – personal ties, shared social norms, and relations that cut across social and economic divides. This type of social capital is likely to create more happiness than associations and relations with people who are exactly like you. Perhaps part of the mystery of Nordic happiness has to do with the way people interact and with whom they interact, and not just how much they interact and spend time together?

The U of age

If you ask people around the world which age group is the happiest, many will point to the young: They have all

6.
As an example, my regular doubles partners at my tennis club include a high-school teacher, an archeologist, a carpenter, and a gardener who takes care of the local churchyard. After our matches, we often sit and have a beer with a cook, a wine merchant, and the marketing director of a large corporation

their lives ahead of them, they have a huge number of different opportunities and paths in life to choose from, and they are at their physical peak. Others, however, will point out the importance of life experience, arguing instead that the elderly may be the happiest, because they have the most experience: The old know themselves much better than the young, they know what "makes them tick" and what they like and do not like, and they also know what to expect from themselves and society, and how to get around obstacles and problems. Only one group is practically never mentioned: the middle-aged.

It is therefore fascinating to note that both arguments are, to some extent, true. In almost all countries where ordinary people have been surveyed, we find that the youngest and the oldest are the happiest. Conversely, the least happy people are typically in their mid-to-late 40s. In other words, happiness studies confirm that the "midlife crisis" is a real, and quite significant, phenomenon for most people. The question is: What happens that leads to lower happiness until the midlife crisis, and what then happens that leads to more happiness after the age of 50?

One of the best explanations of what is going on is that the basic expectations of individuals change over the course of their lives: What they want in their future lives, the plans they make, what job they hope to get, what they expect their body to be able to do ... Everyone harbors more or less explicit expectations of the future, and bases their plans on those expectations. Similarly, everyone has hopes for the future, even though most people do not genuinely expect those hopes to become reality. But gradually, from youth and over the course of the next two decades, many of one's plans and hopes fail to become reality, and one's expectations turn out to be unrealistic. On a personal level, once you reach your 40s, you may face a multitude of objective problems: You may have trouble making the mortgage payments on your house, your teenage children are probably misbehaving, your partner is not as exciting as when you first met, and you may have reached a position at work where promotion is no longer an option.

All of those problems require you to change what you expect from the rest of your life. The Norwegian political scientist Ottar Hellevik once characterized the situation around midlife crisis as the moment when you realize that you'll never make the national soccer team. His insight from studying very detailed Norwegian surveys is that, as part of their midlife crises, people change their basic expectations and their plans for the rest of their lives. As they do so – by adjusting their expectations, figuring out how to do things in a different way than they used to, and making other plans that are more realistic and suitable for the people they have become – they become happier.

Eventually, the association between age and happiness comes to resemble a U shape: The left side of the U is the trip down the curve, from the teenage years until the 40s; the bottom of the U is the midlife crisis, when people go through the painful process of changing their expectations and plans; and the right side is the recovery from this crisis, when people become happier again until they reach old age. What happens when people become very old is still a mystery in happiness research.

Optimism and pessimism

Another major component in most people's lives is the many things they have learned from their parents and grandparents. One of the most important things people learn is optimism versus pessimism: Is the glass half full or half empty? Some children grow up in an encouraging environment where parents believe that if this week was bad, then next week will be better. Other children grow up with parents who do not instill in them a feeling that things are going to get better. These types of basic outlook on life are often perpetuated through family generations, and they are likely to shape people's attitudes for the rest of their lives.

A sense of optimism, or pessimism, turns out to be a key determinant of happiness and life satisfaction. The economist Alan Piper recently showed that in Germany, the effect of being pessimistic about the future is more detrimental to one's life satisfaction than the effect of losing one's job. Theoretically, there are many ways that optimism could affect your life. Minor setbacks are easier to handle when one believes that other parts of life are going to be fine, and optimistic people are therefore more resilient when they encounter minor obstacles and small problems. More optimistic people are also more likely to try new things – buy new goods and services, travel to new places, and consider other ways of doing things – and they therefore learn more about what they like and how best to act in their lives.

Using a question from the Eurobarometer surveys about how positive respondents' overall views of the future are allows us to calculate an "optimism-versus-pessimism" index: all optimists count 1; all pessimists count -1; and adding them up yields a full index from -1 to +1. Doing so for the most recently available years, 2016–2019, shows that both formerly communist countries and other Western countries, on average, score .21, while the three Nordic EU members (Denmark, Finland, and Sweden) average .31. The Eurobarometer data thus reflect what several other surveys have shown: Even though foreigners often think that people in the Nordics appear a little gloomy at times, Nordic natives are typically quite optimistic about the future.

Children will not make you happy

For most people, part of the meaning of life is having children. The picture of a "normal life" in the Nordic countries and large parts of the Western world – or a caricature of it, some would say – is a married couple with a house, two children, and a Volvo in the driveway. When parents are asked about happy moments in their lives, most of them also remember particularly happy moments and situations with their children, including their births. It is therefore somewhat puzzling to note that parents tend to become *less* satisfied with their lives when they have children. Their memories are of moments of short-term happiness, while the long-term happiness or satisfaction of parents is lower than average.

The empirical finding that children make their parents unhappy, or at least less happy, is by far the most unpopular of all findings in happiness research, but also one that has been replicated in study after study across the world. The Norwegian researcher Thomas Hansen has surveyed the literature on happiness and children, and he concludes that parents whose children still live at home are substantially less satisfied with their lives than people of the same age, income, and job who do not have children. It is not having children *per se* that makes people unhappy; it is what happens in their lives for as long as their children live at home. Hansen's finding is also confirmed by studies from several different countries that follow the same people over a number of years. In these studies, where it is possible to see the effects of specific events in people's lives, it is evident that their life satisfaction decreases after having children.

It turns out that at least three effects contribute to the sorry state of many parents. First, all parents worry about their children: Are they healthy? Are they doing well at school? Do they have friends? Are their friends a good influence on them? Are they misbehaving? Can they find a good job? Can they find a nice girlfriend or boyfriend? Are they happy? Parents can think of a million worries, none of which will seem insignificant, but they will, to some extent, disappear – or at least exist only at a distance – when the children leave home.

Second, parents prioritize their children's needs above their own. They may really want to buy a new pair of shoes, attend night school, or go on a vacation abroad, but they will often choose to prioritize buying new shoes for their children or spend their time driving their children to soccer practice instead of going on a weekend getaway. Parents may have needs and wants that do not coincide with those of their children, but still they tend to prioritize the children's needs and suppress their own. Parents very often experience much less freedom in their lives than other people the same age – people they may have grown up with, be friends with, and compare themselves to.

Third, a major related problem for many parents is that they are always parents and never simply a couple. This is not only a matter of what goes on – and does not go on. It is also the problem of not being able to go to the theater on a Friday night – or rather, of a trip to the theater requiring careful long-term planning in the form of hiring a babysitter or convincing grandparents or neighbors to look after the children for an entire evening. This problem gets even worse if the couple plans on having a nice dinner before. the play. There are dozens of such examples that all tell the same basic story: Couples often stop behaving like couples and doing what they used to do as a couple, becoming full-time parents instead. Some of the joys of being a couple therefore easily disappear when one becomes a parent.

Finally, children are expensive. In Western countries, many assessments say that raising a child from birth to the age of 18 typically costs about 200,000 US dollars.

This final factor also constrains the choices of parents and what they can do with their lives. However, none of these effects would be severe if people didn't really care about their children and try their best to create a good life for them. The paradox is that virtually all parents report that they love their children, but this love contributes to their loss of happiness.

Having a job is not a nuisance

Finally, most people spend most of their time outside their home, on the job. Whether the job description is shop clerk, car mechanic, or – in my case – university professor, our jobs are one of the most significant parts of our lives. It is also a part of our lives where folk theory and the insights from happiness studies really clash.

There are many sayings and proverbs about work: "You should work to live, not live to work." "Life starts when you retire." "Life is not what you do, but who you are." Virtually every language and culture has this type of saying, based on the folk theory that working is "a necessary drag" – "Another day, another dollar" – and should be considered a downside and not a benefit in your life. Most cultures simply have a normative bias against the importance of work, and a social norm that mundane things like working to earn an income should not matter to one's personal happiness.

The evidence from happiness studies overwhelmingly rejects these folk-theoretical ideas by showing how important having a job is to the happiness and life satisfaction of most people. The happiness a person loses on losing their job is typically of the same magnitude as the loss caused by a divorce or the death of a life partner. In other words, having a job is one of the most important sources of happiness in most people's lives, even for those who cannot "do what they love, and love what they do."

Considering what everyday life looks like for the average citizen of Norway, Peru, or South Africa, this should come as no surprise. Most of the social relations and social contacts we have outside of our families are often related to our jobs. We meet and interact with colleagues, students, customers, and clients – sometimes developing a truly personal relationship with them – and the many other people we meet through our jobs. Most people also take pride in supporting themselves financially and not having to rely on the help of strangers or the government. Most of us are brought up that way, and even those who are not are conditioned by society to believe that taking care of yourself and not being a burden on other people is the "right thing" to do. This type of work ethic exists all over the world, but it may be strongest in Northern Europe. The German sociologist Max Weber, for example, believed that the strong work ethic he found in Northern Europe was a consequence of Protestantism and its insistence on personal responsibility – in Protestantism, there is no absolution from sin. Yet while Weber was correct that the phenomenon seems to be particularly strong in Northern Europe and its "offspring countries" (Australia, Canada, Hong Kong, New Zealand, and the US), he was probably wrong in regarding Protestantism as the cause. It appears that the individual work ethic is equally strong in the Catholic regions of Southern Germany and in Catholic Belgium as it is in the Protestant regions of North Germany and the Protestant Netherlands. In recent years, an entire literature started by the German economist Ludger Wössman has explored the merits of Weber's hypothesis by using information from nineteenth-century German and Prussian censuses. In general, this literature has questioned Weber's interpretation of the German North–South differences, and therefore also questioned whether the Nordic work ethic is fundamentally different from what one can observe across many other countries.

Finally, the job you do often provides a sense of identity and may also reflect who you are, what you're good at, and your current status and life situation. In Northern cultures in particular, the first questions a stranger you meet at a party is likely to ask you are: "So where are you from? And what do you do for a living?" Your answer – "I'm a carpenter," or "I'm a primary school teacher," or "I'm the captain of a container ship," or, in my case, "I'm a professor" – tells people a bit about who you are and prevents you from being anonymous. And in such situations, many people will use your answer as a chance to get to know you a little better. In other cultures, people instead tend to just ask where you are from, or – as in parts of the United States – which church you frequent.

Having a job-related identity gives many people a meaning in life and may also allow them to avoid being entirely anonymous when they meet other people. Some occupations and professions are considered more prestigious than others, although prestige is probably not as important in social situations in the Nordics as in many other places in the world. Nevertheless, regardless of where people live, it is important to study whether the income they earn on the job is important to their happiness.

Chapter 4.

Can money buy you happiness?

One of the very first questions asked in what would later become "happiness studies" was whether money makes people happier. For centuries, economists from Adam Smith and Karl Marx to Amartya Sen and Friedrich Hayek have expected that a higher income, which enables a person to have an *objectively* better life, would also lead them to *subjectively* perceive their life as better. This idea is built into "utility theory," a mainstay of economic theory that states that higher consumption leads to more "utility" – the standard economic concept that is the closest equivalent to "happiness." It is also an intuitively appealing idea that people will use the resources they have at hand to make their lives better, and that more resources therefore allow them to have better lives. But is it true?

In 1974, the American economist Richard Easterlin challenged this standard economic notion. Easterlin used data from a survey in the US, which asked questions about happiness, to explore whether people actually become happier as they grow richer. His answer was "no": Even though Americans had become much richer in the twenty years prior to 1974, Easterlin's data did not show that they had become happier. For many years, the consensus in happiness studies followed Easterlin's finding that money does not buy happiness.

However, at the beginning of the twenty-first century, several studies began to challenge what, by that time, had become known as "the Easterlin paradox." Ruut Veenhoven, a Dutch sociologist who was one of the first Europeans to take happiness studies seriously, noted that the substantial amounts of data on happiness and life satisfaction that had become available during the 1990s did not seem to support the paradox. Populations in richer countries were clearly more satisfied with their lives than populations in poorer countries, which directly contradicted the Easterlin paradox.

Since then, there has been a lively debate between some researchers who continue to support Easterlin and others who conclude that wealth does, indeed, contribute to greater satisfaction and happiness in the very long run. Two studies from 2008 – one by the later Nobel Prize winner Angus Deaton, and another by the researcher couple Betsy Stevenson and Justin Wolfers – were particularly influential in changing the perception of income. Stevenson and Wolfers showed the existence of two phenomena that seem to be common across the world: People with higher incomes tend to be happier than people in the same society with lower incomes, and societies with higher average incomes tend to be happier than societies with lower average incomes.

Figure 4.1 Average life satisfaction, low to high incomes

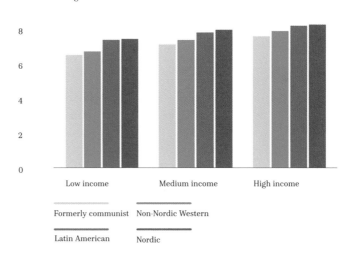

Figure 4.1 Average life satisfaction, low to high incomes

This insight has been central to how income is now seen by most social scientists in happiness research. Based on the data in the seventh wave of the WVS, Figures 4.1 and 4.2 show these differences and provide an impression of how large they are. Figure 4.1 first shows the average life satisfaction among people in this book's four standard country groups, sorted into those with low, medium, and high incomes. Figure 4.2 instead shows how the average income in a society is associated with the average life satisfaction.

In Figure 4.1 it is easy to see how the third of the population with high incomes are more satisfied with their lives than the middle third, and the middle third are more satisfied than the lower third. In formerly communist societies and Western societies outside the Nordics, the high-income group is about 17% (about 1.1 points) more satisfied than the low-income group, while the corresponding difference is about 11% (.8 points) in Latin America and the Nordics. These differences are typical for most studies that explore income differences, regardless of whether one divides people into three income groups or ten (showing deciles), or uses their actual income. Richer individuals and richer households are happier than poorer individuals and poorer households.

However, one of the three theories of happiness and income introduced below implies that whole societies should *not* become happier when people become richer. This calls on us to explore whether that is the case. Figure 4.2 provides an illustration of the pattern that Stevenson and Wolfers found in 2008: With the exception of the Latin American countries, which are obviously outliers, there is a clear association between income and average life satisfaction: In general, richer countries are also happier countries. But the question of why income affects happiness has quite different theoretical answers, depending on the field of research.

Figure 4.2 Average income and life satisfaction *

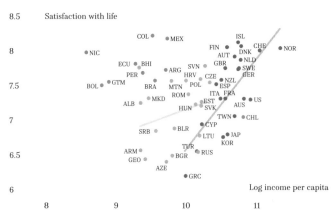

* Note that one purple dot – Chile (CHL) – sits among the olive dots – the Western countries. This is normal for Chile, which an Argentinian colleague once described to me as a European country that happens to be located on the wrong continent

Income

When trying to understand why richer people are happier than poorer people, economics, sociology, and psychology offer three very different theories. Starting with modern economics, the understanding of income and consumption rests on what is known as "utility theory," which was developed from the late nineteenth century onwards. According to utility theory, we become happier as we become richer because our additional resources enable us to buy more of what we think will make our lives better. This may be a new house, a bigger car, or a beautiful Persian rug. However, the money may also enable us to hire a babysitter so we, as parents, can enjoy an evening out, or a cleaner so we don't have to spend our time at home vacuuming the carpets or scrubbing the bathtub.

Yet modern utility theory also tells us that some people may use their additional resources on going on more exciting vacations, or taking more time off: If we earn more per hour we work, we may choose to work fewer hours and have more time off, instead of earning more in total. And when we go on vacation, some of us may become happier after a sunny day on the beach, while others would prefer to spend their money on a mountain hike, and others again would look forward to an evening at the Royal Albert Hall. Because different people can have vastly different preferences, how money is best spent is a very individual matter. Ever since Adam Smith, economic theory has been able to tell us that richer people will, in general, be happier because they have more options – but it is silent when it comes to what people actually do with their money.

An entirely different theory, with different implications and a different explanation of why richer people are happier, comes from sociology, particularly from the work of the American social psychologist Leon Festinger and ideas he developed in the 1950s. Festinger believed that all people compare their material status with a "reference group" of neighbors or friends. Instead of looking at what they actually have, they look at what they have compared to their neighbors; as the saying goes, they want to "keep up with the Joneses." Theoretically, this implies that, all other things being equal, if your car is bigger than your neighbor's car, you are happier. But the day your neighbor gets a bigger car than you, your happiness drops as much as your neighbor's rises, and so on, in a perpetual zero-sum game. This is what sociologists and social psychologists have called the "hedonic treadmill," where we continuously try to satisfy our wants but get nowhere because our friends and neighbors do the same.

Many proponents of Festinger's theory even go a step further by assuming that a thousand dollars will bring more happiness, through greater objective improvements, to those with less money – potentially buying a poor Danish or Norwegian family a season pass to the zoo or a year's worth of guitar lessons, or a poor Australian or Canadian family a better car. The argument is that a wealthier family can already afford these things, so they would spend the money on something else that is objectively less important and would make little difference to them. The important political implication of this version of the theory, which is sometimes known as the "Lerner argument" after the Russian-British socialist economist Abba Lerner, is that redistribution would make society happier as a whole. One would be able to create more happiness by distributing resources away from relatively wealthy people towards less wealthy people, and thereby make the comparative differences smaller. As we shall see later, the evidence for this argument in happiness studies is mixed, at best.

There is another branch of the tradition from Festinger, which holds that people compare themselves with a different "reference" point – not their friends or neighbors, but their own normative perceptions and ideas of what "the good life" ought to be. Most of us have a fairly clear picture of what others, and society, expect from us, and a sort of ideal image of how people like ourselves – our age, with our income, education, job type, or family background – ought to live their lives. This branch of Festinger's comparative theory holds that people's expectations of life, and their own assessments of what they actually have, depend not on what their neighbors have, but on their perceptions of what other people in general have. This perception is thought to be created by the media, such that media reporting on the fortunes of the Kardashians or the glamorous lives of daytime TV stars or basketball players makes reality pale in comparison: The media make people unhappy.

The general message of Festinger's comparative theory, which is quite unlike the picture painted by conventional economic thinking, is therefore this: People are only happier if they are *relatively* richer, compared either to their personal reference group or to some form of society- or media-generated ideal. As Festinger says, if everyone becomes wealthier, which is typical in classic economic development, no one becomes happier: Relative to the Joneses, we remain the same.

However, there is the third theory, which is an alternative to the optimism of standard economic theory and the pessimism of sociological "comparison theory," and which derives from psychology. This theory takes its starting point in the fact that most people have expectations, standards, and a conception of what a "normal life" is, and this is the life with which they compare their own. While the basic ideas of what a normal life ought to be may differ from country to country, the main element in this theory, which is often referred to as either "aspiration theory" or "adaptation theory," is that these expectations and standards are *dynamic*: People adjust their expectations and standards relative to the actual courses their lives take. In other words, while this is a gradual and sometimes slow but continuous process, most people get used to becoming richer or poorer, becoming faster or slower, and becoming older. Unlike in Festinger's comparative theory, individual expectations are not set consciously relative to other people or to the expectations of society, but depend instead on our personal, individual goals, which also adjust over time.

The phrase "adaptation theory" therefore reflects that expectations adapt reasonably to changes in our actual life opportunities. If a B-student suddenly gets an A on an exam, she will be happy because it is more than she expected, just as an A-student becomes unhappy when she receives a B. However, the former B-student who suddenly starts getting A's will, over time, raise her expectations, and the day she expects to get an A, actually getting an A will not make her any happier. Likewise, if a young person has expectations of the salary he can earn in his first job after university, and if these prove too high compared to what is possible or reasonable, he is likely to learn this and – however reluctantly – lower his expectations over time.

In the school of adaptation theory, researchers therefore assume that expectations are not primarily created by society or by direct comparisons to a reference group, but are individual and dynamic. For income and wealth, it follows that this type of theory states that income increases that are *not* expected will make most people happier for a while, but as their expectations rise – as we "raise the bar" on our lives and change our perceptions of what a normal life entails – we slowly fall back towards how happy we were before we received the raise. Adaptation theory therefore argues that economic growth creates happiness, although only for a limited time.

Is income important?

With three different theories that all seek to explain how income may or may not affect happiness and life satisfaction, it can be difficult to assess their respective merits. Fortunately, many studies in happiness economics have gathered data that can contribute to the income debate. The 2008 paper by Stevenson and Wolfers was particularly influential because it documented that standard economic theory must explain at least some of the differences in happiness.

Figure 4.2 illustrates their point: On average, if a Western country becomes twice as rich, average life satisfaction increases by .3 to .4 points. The increase is slightly smaller for formerly communist countries but is still substantially positive. This pattern, which is exactly what Stevenson and Wolfers documented and subsequent studies have confirmed, does not invalidate the two other theories. But it logically shows that standard economic theory must be partially correct – that there are income increases that we do not adapt to fully, and that do not disappear in a hedonic treadmill. To some extent, money can and does buy happiness.

Still, the happiness effects of some objective improvements do disappear over time, as predicted by adaptation theory. In general, it seems to be a feature across countries and cultures that most people overestimate the effects of becoming richer – and of other major life events – because they underestimate how quickly and how much they will adapt to a new situation.[7] Nevertheless, as we shall see just below, there are also some types of consumption that people do not get used to in the usual way. Happiness researchers often quip that the happiness and satisfaction associated with a new car lasts about as long as the "new-car smell." Within a few months, people have gotten used to the new car, even though objectively

7.
Odermatt & Stutzer (2019) is a long-term study of how happy or unhappy subjects expected to become after marrying, divorcing, becoming disabled, or losing a partner. Reports from subjects who later experienced these life events were compared with their own earlier predictions. Most respondents were found to "mispredict" the effects; for example, they overestimate the happiness they would derive from marriage, or underestimate how quickly they would adapt to losing a partner

it may be a much better car than their old one. In other words, they have changed their perception of a "normal car" and are therefore not happier in the long run than they were with the old car.

Income inequality

As for the second theory, comparison theory, the supporting evidence is somewhat weaker. There are good reasons to suspect that people do compare their lives to their friends' and neighbors', but there are also good reasons to believe that reference groups change over time. In other words, just as one's expectations are dynamic and change throughout one's life, one's reference group also changes: You don't keep comparing yourself to Poor Old Pete in your favorite pub if you become twice as wealthy. Likewise, if you're an avid soccer fan, your happiness will probably not suffer from comparing your humble abilities to those of the Argentinian superstar Lionel Messi, because the comparison is so obviously ridiculous. The dynamics of people's reference groups makes it very difficult to test how much comparison theory can tell us.

However, a particular and politically popular interpretation of Festinger's comparison theory has been tested a number of times in the literature (Alesina, DiTella, & MacCulloch 2004; Berg & Veenhoven 2010). This is the interpretation that holds that redistribution should make average citizens happier, so that countries such as Brazil, South Africa, or the United Kingdom, which have more unequally distributed incomes, ought to be less happy. It is therefore also a version of comparison theory that is easy to test, because relatively good data on income inequality are available for most countries in the world.

In general, these tests nevertheless reject the idea that income inequality is clearly associated with happiness or life satisfaction. First, had income inequality been a powerful determinant of happiness, one would have expected the differences between low- and high-income people in Figure 4.2 to be particularly large in Latin America, which is known to have some of the most unequal distributions of income in the world. However, Latin American differences are about the same as in the Nordics, which have extremely low income inequality. The non-association is also visible in Figure 4.3, where I combine the most recent measures of inequality in disposable income – that is, the income that people actually have at their disposal after paying taxes and tariffs and receiving income transfers and subsidies – and plot them against the differences in life satisfaction between low-income and high-income citizens in the WVS. Most evidence suggests that there is no clear association between income inequality and life satisfaction. However, this remains one of the most heated discussions in happiness research, and one which continues to result in new studies that find evidence supporting negative effects, positive effects, and no effects.

Figure 4.3 Inequality and satisfaction differences between low-income and high-income citizens

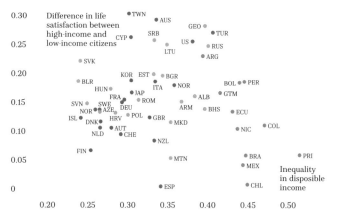

How do you spend your money?

While income inequality seems to be irrelevant to happiness, there are other complications with respect to income. As noted above, standard economic theory tells us little about which kinds of consumption will make people happier. But how people spend their income actually matters in terms of how much happiness they derive from that consumption.

First, several studies from Western countries suggest that money spent on "experience consumption" – visits to the theater, hiking in the mountains, football games, or some other form of experience – yield much more lasting happiness than money spent on things (Gilovich, Kumar, & Jampol 2015). In other words, the adaptation to experiences is slower than the adaption to material things, such as a new car. If money spent on experiences yields more lasting happiness, that would also explain why rich people are typically happier: The structure of people's consumption changes with wealth, so that the wealthier people become, the larger a share of their income is spent on experiences.

However, although some of the most recent studies find that consumption is much more important than income, they have also questioned whether experience consumption is particularly important. Some of the effects from experiences may be short-lived, and which kind of consumption makes you happy may depend on your personality type. At least one of the new studies finds, instead, that money spent on vacations may be more important for some people, while for others money spent on clothing has a greater effect on their happiness.[8] Essentially, this is one of the questions where earlier studies seemed to provide clear answers, but where larger and more recent studies have made researchers realize that what we thought we knew may not be true.

8. Kumara, Killingsworth, & Gilovich (2020) showed that short-lived happiness is linked more to experience consumption than to consumption of material goods. However, recent work by Gordon Brown and John Gathergood has found that while spending on vacations and hobbies is most effective in raising happiness, the effects of experience consumption are less clear-cut

44

Second, another insight comes from the fact that most people prefer to avoid risk and are consequently prepared to pay substantial amounts to insurance companies. It is therefore not surprising that evidence from such different countries as Sweden, Turkey, and the UK shows that people with more savings are more satisfied with their lives. This is also eminently intuitive and easy to understand: If you have savings in the bank, it will not affect your everyday life if your dishwasher breaks down. You simply pay a repairman or buy a new dishwasher using your savings, because that's what they are for. If you hadn't had any money saved up, your life would have been more difficult.

How do you earn your income?

A final complication regarding income is that while having a job is extremely important for how satisfied most people are with their lives, it may also matter how people earn their income. Observations indicate that the happiness effect of income may depend on how one earns that income, but many questions still remain unanswered. For example, the effects of the size of unemployment benefits and pensions are uncertain and difficult to assess. Without very detailed information about how large people's public pensions, private pension plans, and savings are, it becomes almost impossible to assess their effects. Similarly, the effects of potentially having access to unemployment benefits are extremely difficult to assess, because certain personality factors and other differences among people make some happier and less likely to become unemployed. Whether the Nordic welfare policies and comprehensive "social safety nets" make any difference in individuals' happiness is therefore uncertain.

There are, however, at least two features related to jobs and to how one earns one's income that we can describe with reasonable certainty. First, jobs with more social contacts tend to generate more job satisfaction and, by extension, more satisfaction with life. All other things being equal, we would therefore expect teachers, journalists, and lifeguards to be happier than farmers, truck drivers, or cooks. In general, as Jan-Emmanuel De Neve and George Ward showed in a theme chapter in the 2017 *World Happiness Report*, blue-collar workers are typically less happy than white-collar workers because blue-collar jobs create less on-the-job happiness than white-collar jobs.

The value of social relations and the other non-monetary benefits of having a job was elegantly illustrated by Bruno Frey and Alois Stutzer. These two Swiss economists, who are both pioneers of the economics of happiness, combined information about how much satisfaction people lose when losing their job, and how much satisfaction money can buy. In doing so, they calculated that for public unemployment benefits to ensure that people did not become less satisfied when they lost their jobs, the benefits would have to be approximately 350% of the income they used to earn in their old job. Unemployment benefits that are 3.5 times higher than a normal wage is obviously a ridiculous notion, but the example illustrates quite nicely how large a happiness benefit most people enjoy from their job, which has nothing to do with the income they earn.

Another difference appears to be the nature of one's employment. Bruno Frey observed almost twenty years ago that people across the world who are self-employed are happier than other people with the same income. This observation has been intensely discussed since then, but it remains poorly understood. However, the increase in happiness observed on becoming self-employed is known to exist only when the change is voluntary. It is also unlikely to apply to everyone, as choosing to become self-employed only appeals to people with very specific preferences and competence profiles.

These research questions are at the frontier of happiness studies. While it is clear that having a job is extremely important for most people, and that income and consumption do make a difference – regardless of popular beliefs and social norms – many more detailed questions are left unanswered. They are difficult to answer and often require more information about people's private finances than is available to researchers, but they are also currently the focus of many academic efforts. Fortunately, we know much more about the next topic, which is the institutional framework that affects both economic incentives and life satisfaction for everyone.

Chapter 5.
Good institutions go a long way

Over the last thirty years, economists and political scientists have documented the importance of institutions for long-term economic and societal development. The Nobel laureate Douglass North famously defined institutions as "the humanly devised constraints that structure political, economic, and social interactions." For North, examples of formal institutions are the judiciary and the police along with the legislation they enforce, and the public bureaucracy and the regulations it implements. The formal institutional framework also includes the degree to which politics are democratic, and the type of democracy or autocracy a country, state, or region has. Many economists and political scientists therefore distinguish between "political institutions" and "other institutions," the latter including the courts and the police, the scope and quality of regulations, and the public bureaucracy.

It is easy to see how good institutions contribute to "the good life," and a whole string of studies document that life satisfaction is closely related to the quality of institutions.[9] However, different institutions contribute in

9.
A literature review I recently conducted with Niclas Berggren found almost 100 large-scale empirical studies exploring the links between happiness/life satisfaction and institutions (about two thirds look at judicial/bureaucratic institutions; about one third at political institutions)

different ways, and the effects of democracy are different from those of good judicial institutions.

Democracy and happiness

Let us begin by looking at the WVS data summarized in the columns in Figure 5.1, which illustrates that democracies are generally happier than autocracies: The average life satisfaction in democracies is 7.35, while it is 6.72 in autocracies. However, one has to be careful when interpreting this difference, because democracies also tend to be richer than autocracies. Some of the additional happiness in democracies could arise because they are richer, or because democracies have better "other" institutions, beyond their political institutions.

Figure 5.1 Democracy and happiness

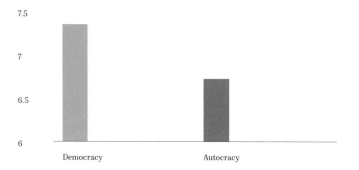

8   Average life satisfaction

However, most studies find that when countries become more democratic, this does make their citizens happier in the long run. The effect of having democratic political institutions may nevertheless only apply to societies that are sufficiently rich. As emphasized by the Dutch happiness specialist Jan Ott, it seems that people need to be wealthy enough, and sufficiently far from deep poverty, before they start to value the degree of political influence offered by modern democracy.

In other words, when people live in absolute poverty with a real risk of not being able to buy enough food from day to day, their life satisfaction is not affected by which political system they live under. When they are able to put such worries behind them, they start valuing democracy. Democracy is therefore an important source of happiness in middle-income and affluent countries such as the Nordics. The next question is, therefore, *how* democracy and democratic political institutions make people happier and more satisfied with their lives.

Frey and Stutzer have devoted several studies to this question. They note that democracy can affect people's life satisfaction in two different ways: through better outcomes, and through what they call "procedural utility." First, democracy could lead to objectively better outcomes, or to decisions and outcomes that better match most people's preferences. Second, procedural utility is the satisfaction people derive from knowing (or believing) that decisions are made in a fair, balanced, and democratic manner – that the *process* through which decisions are reached is just.

Several researchers, including Frey himself, have gone a step further and argued that direct democracy – a type of democracy where many important issues are decided by public referenda – makes people even happier, and that this is a major reason why Switzerland is among the world's happiest countries. This argument also rests on the idea that direct democracy results in decisions that suit most people better, not least because they are directly involved in decision-making. However, Frey and Stutzer's Swiss colleague Isabelle Stadelmann-Steffen suggests that direct democracy is primarily associated with life satisfaction because it makes most people more satisfied with democracy per se.

Stadelmann-Steffen therefore suggests that the effect of direct democracy is probably more related to procedural utility, as direct involvement feels fairer for most people. This is also reflected in the degree to which people in the Nordic countries are satisfied with how democracy works. In responses to that question in the EuroBarometer, the Nordics typically share the top spots, together with Luxembourg and the Netherlands. As far as can be judged from such surveys, the populations in the Nordics are particularly satisfied with some feature particular to Nordic democracy. Yet it remains an open question whether this is just a reflection of other factors that make the Nordics happier, or a consequence of having a democratic choice between many parties instead of just two – or whether the Nordic satisfaction with democracy has to do with something entirely different.

Quite apart from this, as in the case of happiness and income, there are also many open questions about happiness and democracy. Democracy comes in many forms – with one or two chambers of parliament; based on proportional voting, as is common in the Nordics, or on "first past the post" systems, as in the UK and the US; as presidential or parliamentary regimes; as unitary or federal systems; and with more or less systematic involvement with civil society – and relatively little is known about the importance of these details. One could speculate that the tradition of minority government and consensus democracy in Denmark, Finland, and Norway could contribute to their happiness, but the honest answer is that this too remains an open question.

Judicial and bureaucratic institutions

While there is evidence to suggest that democracy is only relevant for happiness in countries that are "rich enough," a wide range of studies document that the quality of judicial and bureaucratic institutions is equally important in rich and poor societies. These types of institutions include a number of authorities and bodies that ordinary people often interact with during the course of their lives. In countries where the judicial and bureaucratic institutions fail to work properly, people have to manage life with a poorly functioning police force, widespread corruption in the public bureaucracy, and courts and other judicial institutions that are slow, biased, and influenced by political interference. It is therefore easy to see how the quality of these institutions and the degree to which they uphold what is commonly called "the rule of law" is central to how satisfied an entire population can be. Their crucial role is illustrated in Figure 5.2, which shows the clear association between the rule of law and life satisfaction. Incidentally, this figure also shows that the Nordics and Switzerland have some of the finest judicial institutions in the world. But just as democracy can have two different effects, judicial and bureaucratic institutions can also affect happiness in different ways.

Figure 5.2 Happiness and the rule of law

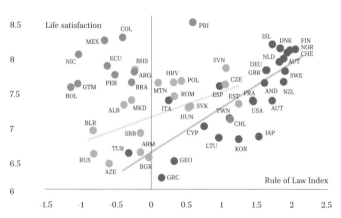

The obvious ways in which good institutions can affect happiness and life satisfaction are easy to imagine, as also described above. Good judicial institutions and an effective police force, for example, protect people's lives in two different ways. First, they reduce the overall level of crime in a country, such that everyone's lives and property are safer. As noted before, people in general do not like risk and are willing to pay to reduce the element of risk in their lives. With good institutions, such risks are smaller and this therefore reduces the constant need either to insure oneself or to change one's behavior in order to avoid risks.

Having access to good institutions also reduces the consequences of a crime for victims who are robbed, burgled, or threatened, for instance. The chances that a crime will be solved are much higher when the police works well, and the chances that criminals will be convicted, stolen property returned, or the victims compensated in some way are much higher when the judicial institutions work properly. Conversely, when these institutions do not work properly and effectively – for example because police officers, bureaucrats, or judges can be bribed, or simply cannot be held accountable for poor behavior – the consequences for crime victims are much worse. These can be considered the "direct effects" of having access to good institutions that uphold law and order.

However, good institutions can also affect life satisfaction in another way that resembles the "procedural utility" created by democracy. This "indirect effect" comes about because good institutions also give people a sense of living in a fair and just society. For almost everyone, the feeling of living in a fair society is important to the way they perceive their lives, although what a person considers to be "fair" can vary substantially. Nevertheless, the value of good institutions in the form of fair and effective courts, a trustworthy and efficient police force, and an uncorrupt, impartial public bureaucracy – like those that have characterized the Nordics, and also Australia and New Zealand, for a century – is one of the things that people tend to agree on. And having objectively good institutions also means that people perceive society to be "fair" even when those institutions have to make hard decisions to protect everyone's lives, property, and civil rights.

Confidence in institutions

An entirely different way of approaching the importance of institutions, and one that can capture some of these intangible, individual perceptions, relies on exploring how much confidence individuals have in different institutions. Instead of trying to measure the *objective* quality of institutions like the police, courts, public bureaucracy, or the political system, one can ask people about their *subjective* assessment of them. This approach, which was pioneered in happiness studies by the Canadian economist John Helliwell, therefore relies on what really matters for most people: their own perception of what is going on.

It nevertheless yields very similar findings, although it also reveals that even in countries with good institutions, individuals can have widely different opinions about them. Using another example from the WVS, it turns out that people who have some or a lot of confidence in the courts and the judicial system are happier than those who do not. Among Western countries, people with confidence in the courts are about 6% (.4 points) more satisfied with their lives than those with no confidence. The same is the case in formerly communist countries, while the difference is slightly larger in the Nordic countries (7% or .5 points) and smaller in Latin America (3% or .2 points). These differences therefore help us understand why the Nordic populations are happier than the rest of the world: There are 16% more people who have confidence in the courts in the Nordics than in the rest of the Western world, and double as many as in formerly communist countries. In these countries, contrary to many other places, the police, courts, and civil servants are not seen as faceless personal threats, but as establishments full of other people who are there to help.[10]

Summing up, one of the really important differences between countries in the world, which makes some of them much happier than others, is the quality of their institutions. In middle- and high-income countries, democracy makes people happier, although very little is known about which type of democracy – if any – is more likely to create happiness. People are also much happier in countries with relatively good judicial and bureaucratic institutions, and while the effect of having such institutions is common to the poorest and the richest countries and individuals, the Nordic countries exhibit some of the most effective judicial institutions in the world. Some of this effect comes about because people in the Nordics have confidence in their institutions – they trust their judges, bureaucrats, and police officers to do their jobs properly, impartially, and effectively. It turns out, however, that our general level of trust in other people is even more important.

10. Across regions, the differences in people's confidence in institutions reflect the differences in objectively measured institutional quality. The average WVS rates, on a 1–4 scale, for confidence in courts and legal institutions are: in Latin America, 1.81; in formerly communist countries, 2.23; in Western countries, 2.68; and in the Nordics, 2.95

Chapter 6.

How does trust contribute to happiness?

Most people, whether they live in Cape Town, Lima, Moscow, or Seattle, trust their family and friends, but there are surprising differences in how much people trust strangers, known by social scientists as "social trust." One of the most important ways in which the Nordics differ from the rest of the world – and one of the differences that is most difficult to see – is in their high levels of social trust. Trust is easy to ignore when one is trying to assess other people and other places, because it is not a physical attribute or a tangible thing, but a belief about how benevolent and trustworthy other people are, which is hidden in our hearts and minds. As a fairly concrete example, however, tourists driving through the Danish countryside in summer often spot small stands by the wayside. These stands typically offer berries, carrots, honey, and other items, mainly edibles, for sale. The prices are clearly advertised, but the stands are unmanned and customers are expected to simply put their payment in a cigar box or a jam jar – or pay with their mobile phone – then drive off with their purchases. These stands are a classic feature of rural Denmark in summertime, and no one else in Scandinavia considers them exceptional. Such stands also exist in Canada, the state of Maine, Oxfordshire, and various other places, but they are rare in the rest of the world.

Unmanned produce stands reflect the extremely high levels of social trust and civic honesty in the Nordic countries. Social trust, defined as the degree of trust you place in other people you do not know, is typically measured using a simple question: "In general, do you think most people can be trusted, or do you have to be careful?" In recent years, when given only two options – the choice of saying either that they "trust most people" or that they "have to be careful" – as in the WVS or the European Values Study, almost 75% of respondents in Denmark and Norway stated that most people can be trusted, while Swedes and Finns were close to 70%. People in Iceland are usually slightly less trusting, with recent surveys showing an average around 65%. The Nordic levels of trust must be compared to the European and global averages, which are both below 30%, and to extreme cases such as Brazil, Peru, and the Philippines, where fewer than 10% of respondents in surveys believe that most people in their societies can be trusted.

One might say it is impossible to compare the Nordic countries with places such as Brazil or the Philippines because the countries and cultures are simply too different. However, even respondents in Denmark's southern neighbor, Germany, are split on the issue of social trust. For example, the WVS shows that in former West Germany, just under 40% of those surveyed state that they trust most other people, while in former East Germany, a communist system until 1990, the corresponding figure is only 25%. For Europe as a whole, just three out of ten respondents – 30% – say that they trust other people, making the Nordics as a region the world's most trusting place. And as it turns out, these high levels of social trust are neither naive nor inconsequential. Evidence shows that the Nordic region has a large majority of extremely honest, decent citizens – who remember to pay for their strawberries.

Two experimental studies, conducted two decades apart, reveal how social trust is reflected in how honestly people behave. At the end of the 1990s, the American monthly *Reader's Digest* pioneered this approach by buying a number of wallets, filling them with cash corresponding to a day's wages, a driving license, and some form of official ID, then "dropping" them in cities in 33 countries. Until then, trust experiments had only been conducted with students, but the purpose of Eric Felton's article, entitled "Finders keepers?" and published in *Reader's Digest*, was to see, in a real-life scenario, how many wallets would actually be returned to their owners with the contents intact. Of the 33 countries, Denmark and Norway were the only places where all wallets were returned with their contents intact. In other wealthy Western countries, including the UK, Germany, and the Netherlands, about half of the wallets disappeared, and in Lisbon only one wallet out of 12 was returned. This pattern was confirmed by a similar study led by Alain Cohn and conducted in 2018 in 355 cities in 40 countries around the world. In the article "Civic honesty around the world," which was published in 2019 in the prestigious journal *Science*, Cohn showed how the three Scandinavian countries – Denmark, Norway, and Sweden – are joined by Switzerland as the countries in which a lost wallet is most likely to be returned to its owner. Both studies therefore show that Nordic social trust is not naive: People in the Nordics typically behave honestly, even in real life.

Trust makes people more satisfied

Their high levels of trust are one of the main explanations why the Nordic countries all rank among the happiest societies in the world. Practically everywhere social scientists have surveyed people, those who believe that "most people can be trusted" are happier than those who think that "you need to be careful." I illustrate this difference between what I call "trusters" and "non-trusters" in Figure 6.1, which shows how, in Western countries, the former are .53 points more satisfied with their lives than the latter, while the difference is .42 in countries with a communist past. While approximately half a point may seem like a small difference, it is comparable to the typical satisfaction difference between married and divorced people, and almost as large as the difference between being married or cohabiting and being a single-person household. As a long list of studies has shown since 2003, being able to trust most other people makes a very substantial difference in a person's life.[11]

11.
The first studies were Helliwell (2003) and Bjørnskov (2003). Helliwell showed that more trusting individuals were happier, while I showed that individuals living in more trusting societies were happier

Figure 6.1 Life satisfaction among "trusters" and "non-trusters"

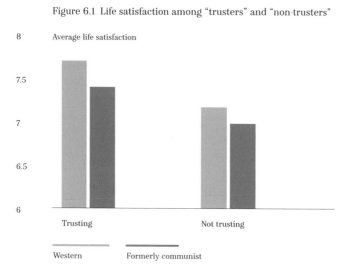

The connection with a happy life is easy to make. In the Nordic countries, if you need to use the restroom while on a train or in a restaurant, it is common either to simply leave your bag on your seat, or to ask a perfect stranger if they would mind keeping an eye on your bag and laptop for the next five minutes. Nordic people evidently worry more about someone taking their seat or table while they are away than the risk that their bag, laptop, or shopping will be stolen. In most of the rest of the world, the risk of theft is the main worry.

Similarly, having trust in strangers makes us happier for several other reasons. Think of an ordinary day in your own life, and you will quickly realize how often you depend on other people, outside your own immediate sphere of family and close friends. We shop for groceries and buy things from people we do not know and may never meet again, yet we are confident they have treated our foodstuffs appropriately and provided the correct "Best before" date while weighing and packaging the items correctly. As we pay the checkout assistant, we hold out cash others could easily grab, or tap in a PIN code that other people could easily note down before stealing our card and dashing away to empty our bank account. Likewise, in many work-related situations we must trust employees from other companies, anonymous customers we will never meet, or representatives of different state authorities – without any opportunity to verify that they really are who they claim to be.

The modern way of life constantly forces us to rely on nameless others, somewhere out there, doing their jobs properly and honestly. If we could not trust most of those strangers most of the time, everyday life would become very difficult. Reflecting on our ordinary daily interactions thereby clearly illustrates the life challenge that the Russian playwright Chekhov has the young Yelena express in a well-known line from Uncle Vanya: "You must believe in people or life will become impossible." Vanya refuses to trust anyone, and by doing so makes his own life impossible, because it means he can never relate normally to other people.

Once you start considering normal life in this way, an amazing number of situations in our modern world prove to be dependent on strangers we may never even see. The more we trust others, and the farther our trust reaches out to people who are not like us, the more protected we are from worries we might harbor. The trick is that, as long as their trust is well-reasoned, people have almost no reason to worry in high-trust societies.

Trust makes societies happier

If this was only about individual differences, the most trusting societies would have average levels of life satisfaction that were about half a point higher than the least trusting societies. However, as is evident in Figure 6.2, which plots the level of social trust against how satisfied the average citizen is, the differences across societies are clearly much larger than the differences across individual citizens. The least trusting societies in the Western world, such as Greece or Portugal, have satisfaction levels of around 6.5, while the most trusting societies reach average levels slightly above 8. It thus seems that social trust is much more important for happiness at the societal level than at the purely individual level. In other words, the degree to which citizens believe that their compatriots can be trusted shapes how the entire society functions, and it does so in a way that increases happiness for everyone.

Research is beginning to understand how a trust culture affects entire societies. One of the obvious ways this happens is through personal interactions: People affect each other's lives in all societies through the way they behave, and in high-trust societies, most people also behave honestly. People who live in the Nordics are embedded in a population where the vast majority are trusting and honest towards others, whether they know them or not. So even though you might be an old curmudgeon who trusts nobody, in a Nordic society you are living among a high-trust population that is unlikely to try to take advantage of you. You might still worry a lot, but your worries are much less likely to become reality in Finland or Norway than in Albania or Peru. In other words, the fact that most people are trusting and trustworthy spills over into the lives of those who are not trusting. Again according to WVS data, non-trusters in high-trust Norway are, on average, just as satisfied with their lives as trusters in low-trust France.

High-trust individuals also behave differently in many other ways, and their attitude and actions in their own lives and towards others generates happiness. That is why trust indirectly contributes to general happiness, as high-trust people are also more inclined to do volunteer work for charities, associations, socially inclusive sports clubs, and so forth. Work of this sort – which they do because they fundamentally believe that other people are decent and honest – gives them access to many more, and more diverse and "class-blind" social relations than others have. Low-trust people, on the other hand, often find it hard to engage socially with people they do not know, which puts them at greater risk of social isolation.

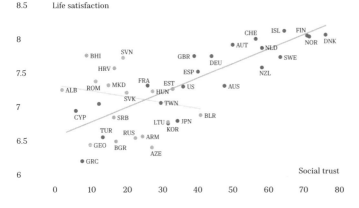

Figure 6.2 Social trust and life satisfaction, two groups

A further effect of trust is that young people who trust others are more likely to get an education. In the late 1980s, the American sociologist James Coleman demonstrated how trust in others reduced high-school dropout rates. Trusting people are easier to work with, and they are therefore more likely to get help with their homework, take part in social events, and get on well with their peers. One of many insights from the last two decades of trust research is that trust is rewarded with trust, fostering honesty and helpfulness.[12] For young people in school or college, the help they can earn by showing trust may be decisive. Trusting behavior also pays off on the bottom line, in the workplace and on the labor market, as trusting people often earn more, firstly because they are better educated, and secondly because they are better at cooperating.

At a broader level, a culture of trust (or distrust) can have even more important consequences, shaping people's lives through its effect on the quality of society's basic institutions – the judiciary, police, public bureaucracy, and the political system – in ways that eventually increase happiness. As we saw in the last chapter on institutions, fair and

12.
Coleman (1988) was one of the first to document the many consequences of social trust, informal networks, and strong communal norms. Nobel laureate Elinor Ostrom pioneered the recognition of trust reciprocity as important to community outcomes. See, e.g., Ostrom & Walker (2003)

64

effective judicial institutions make everyone happier. A great deal of literature, which began with Robert Putnam's seminal book *Making Democracy Work* in 1993, documents how social trust makes such institutions work better. Another Nordic oddity that is far from surprising when one understands how trust affects institutions is that bribery is almost non-existent, unlike in most other regions in the world. People in all of the Nordic countries regularly complain about how the public bureaucracy works, yet their complaints would be considered minor misdemeanors almost anywhere else in the world. Citizens in the Nordic countries enjoy some of the finest judicial institutions in the world and participate in some of the most competitively democratic political systems, all of which, to a large extent, are the result of the Nordic culture of trust.

Overall, extremely high levels of social trust are one of the most important explanations for why the Nordic countries are among the happiest societies in the world. Both through individual behavior and through the way these high trust levels affect the formal institutions that govern society, the culture of trust contributes to making people much happier. Tellingly, according to the 2018 Gallup-Sharecare Well-Being Index, the happiest US states are Minnesota and the Dakotas – along with Hawaii and New Hampshire. The first three states differ from the rest of the US because of the large proportion of their population who can trace their ancestry back to Scandinavia – to such an extent that Scandinavians often mistake Minnesotans for Swedes speaking English – and the way the culture of trust within that population shapes life in their particular part of the Midwest. As a growing literature shows, this culture of trust is not designed or enforced by any particular policy or government action. It is pure luck – but a stroke of pure luck that is sustained through families and traditions that are specific to the Nordics.[13]

13.
Several studies in recent years have documented how ancestry and family origins shape social trust and social norms. See Uslaner (2008) and Sanandaji (2015)

Chapter 7.

Nordic freedom and tolerance

Not everyone is alike; people come in all shapes and sizes, and with all sorts of preferences and interests. If people were alike, we would all lead identical lives and not need any freedom to deviate from what other people do. However, because people are different, their personal freedom to decide what to do with their lives, and also the control they have over their lives, is a central determinant for how satisfied they are.

One of the challenges researchers face when trying to estimate the importance of freedom in people's lives is that freedom can be considered as both an *objective* factor and a *subjective* factor. The objective factor is the question of whether there are laws or regulations that restrict what people are formally allowed to do with their lives. One obvious example is that most countries had laws against homosexuality well into the post-war period, which meant that men with homosexual preferences were effectively excluded from living in a way that suited them, or alternatively had to live their lives secretly.[14] In other countries, until relatively recently, certain occupations and participation in some parts of civil society were closed to

14.
In most countries, male homosexuality was illegal for a long period, while female homosexuality was not. The UK, for instance, did not decriminalize the former until 1966. Other bans on certain behaviors also seem to have been gendered and may have affected men and women differently

people who did not belong to the majority religion. Similarly, in many autocracies and in practically all communist regimes, many occupations and positions are closed to people without a party membership, and occasionally even to people with a membership card but without sufficiently documented loyalty to the party.

The subjective factor is how people perceive the freedom they have to choose the lives they wish to lead. That can, of course, be affected by their objective freedom, but is also influenced by a number of other factors, not least other people's social norms and tolerance towards other, different choices. As such, the subjective aspect of freedom is not a matter of whether one is legally allowed to lead a particular life, but whether one's surroundings – family, friends, colleagues, neighbors, and so on – accept and tolerate one's choices in life.

Objective freedom

"Objective freedom" is related to the quality of a country's institutions and the contents of its laws and legislation. As noted above, such laws may restrict the legality of the preferred life choices of certain sexual, religious, and ethnic minorities. However, the potential effect of such legal restrictions on people's actual opportunities depends on the degree to which they are enforced. Denmark, for example, had a formal ban on blasphemy until 2017, but the last time this ban was actually enforced was in 1937. Conversely, most national constitutions ban discriminatory legislation and behavior, but in many countries the government is nonetheless able to ignore the constitution and ignore, condone, or even practice discrimination.

The fact that, in some countries, the formal legislation can be a far cry from what is enforced by the courts and public bureaucracies makes it very difficult to assess how important such constraints are for the personal freedom of their citizens. This is also why, for most populations, there is precious little evidence of any effects of discriminatory legislation. As we shall see below, however, there is evidence that specific legislation directed against minorities has an effect on life satisfaction.

Subjective freedom

Turning to "subjectively perceived freedom" – how much freedom people feel they have to make their own life choices – measurement is also fraught with difficulty. However, happiness research has made progress on this problem by way of the different approaches to asking about individual perceptions of freedom used by sociologists and political scientists. In the WVS, respondents are asked directly: "How much control do you have over your life?" This question goes directly to the degree to which people subjectively perceive they can make their own life choices without being constrained by either legislation or binding social norms and intolerance. The alternative approach is taken by the GWP, in which respondents are instead asked whether they are satisfied or dissatisfied with the freedom they have to choose what to do with their lives. Much like the GWP question about life satisfaction, discussed earlier, this question asks respondents to relate their subjective personal freedom to some ideal they would like to achieve.

Whichever approach one uses, it is clear that individual happiness is closely related to how individuals perceive their personal freedom. Happiness at an individual level is illustrated in Figure 7.1, which again plots data from the WVS to show the association between perceptions of freedom and control, and individual life satisfaction. In all four regions, people who state that they have substantial control over their lives (a score above 5 on a 1–10 scale) are approximately 30% happier than those who state that they have little control over their lives (a score below 6). Across the world, people with strong freedom perceptions are happier, as they believe that they can choose lives that fit their preferences, expectations, and aspirations, and act to achieve their wishes.

Figure 7.1 Control of life and happiness, individual level

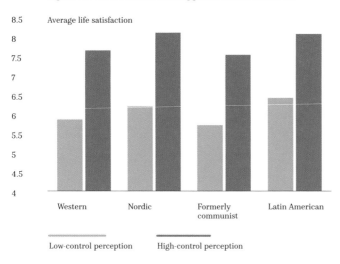

The same picture is replicated across entire nations in Figure 7.2, which reveals the association between average levels of perceived freedom and average life satisfaction. This is the most unambiguous figure in the entire book, and it shows one of the strongest correlations found in recent happiness studies: Everywhere in the world, across countries at different levels of development and with very different histories, citizens' perceptions of freedom in their lives shapes how happy their societies are. It is also one of the few instances in which life satisfaction across Latin American countries does *not* look different from the rest of the world.

This is also, evidently, one of the secrets behind Nordic happiness: The populations of Denmark, Iceland, Finland, and Norway have some of the strongest freedom perception scores of all, with Sweden lagging a little behind, matching the general pattern that the Swedes are the least happy of the Nordic peoples. It also provides some insight into why the Latin American countries are happier than one would think. People's average assessment of control over their own lives in the WVS is 7.79 in Latin American countries and 7.73 in the Nordics. However, for the GWP question about satisfaction with the freedom one has to choose one's life, the Latin American average is .83 while the Nordic average is .95.

Figure 7.2 Perceptions of freedom and happiness, national level

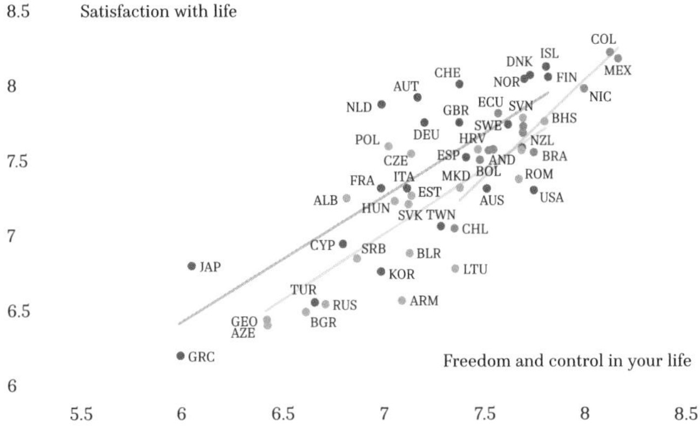

What do we know about minorities?

One of the ways to assess how important freedom perceptions *and* objective obstacles to freedom are is to explore the happiness or life satisfaction of minorities. One specific study does so by using what is known as the "Gay Happiness Index." This index was gathered through a survey of homosexual men in more than 130 countries, who responded online. The resulting data now allows researchers to assess whether this particular minority is as happy as the majority population.

Most importantly for the question of whether objective freedom affects happiness, this index can be read

71

alongside measures for legislation that restricts or pro-
tects the freedom of this particular minority, gay men.
Figure 7.3 illustrates this approach by plotting the life satisfaction data from the Gay Happiness Index relative to a
measure of the legal protection of equal rights for homosexual citizens, as set out in the "ILGA."[15] This index cap-
tures whether homosexuality is legally allowed and consti-
tutionally protected, and whether homosexual citizens
have four specific civil rights that other people regularly
enjoy, as noted below. It is therefore a measure of *objective*
freedom for a specific minority.

Figure 7.3 Gay life satisfaction and legal recognition

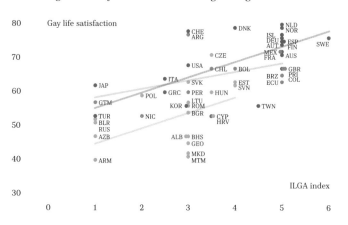

15.
The "ILGA index" is
based on informa-
tion from the report
State Sponsored
Homophobia, from
the International
Lesbian, Gay,
Bisexual, Trans and
Intersex Associa-
tion. It is a version
of the measure used
in the article Berg-
gren, Bjørnskov,
& Nilsson (2017).
As far as we know,
this work remains
the only effort of
its kind

As the figure makes evident, for homosexual men,
objective legal recognition is an important source of life
satisfaction. The right to practice their sexuality, marry,
and adopt children, and formal laws against employers
considering very private characteristics such as sexuality
in employment decisions – which involves establishing
equal rights – make them happier. The data also replicate
a pattern that should be well known by now: The average
happiness among gay men in formerly communist coun-

tries is 52; in Latin America it is 64; in Western countries, 66; and in the Nordics, it is 72.

The other minority that has been investigated in happiness studies is immigrants. Several recent studies show that immigrants' happiness and life satisfaction is typically determined by the exact same factors as people who were born in their new home country (Arpino & de Valk 2018). In other words, what makes the "long-time" inhabitants of a country happier also makes "new arrivals" happier. This implies that immigrants who move from poor to rich countries tend to become substantially happier, as they move to societies with substantially better institutions and much better economic opportunities. Similarly, even when people migrate between rich countries, they often become happier when moving, for example, from a low-trust country to a high-trust country. As noted in Chapter 6, living among a high-trust population makes most people happier, even if they do not share that trust.

Even so, several new studies suggest that immigrants also bring cultural features and traditions with them from home, which continue to shape the life satisfaction of the first generation. Many ways of doing things, basic beliefs about life and society, and social norms are learned early in life, and first-generation immigrants bring these norms and customs to their new country. Their children, who are second-generation immigrants, conversely tend to become so similar to their peers with native parents that one cannot see any difference in their happiness levels. Adaptation to a new country therefore seems to take a generation, and even when migrants move to a substantially happier society, they rarely become as happy as fellow citizens who were born there. Using the findings of one of the most recent studies on this topic, a person migrating from France to one of the Nordic countries – someone moving from a rich, institutionally well-functioning low-trust country to an equally rich, institutionally well-functioning high-trust country – will, over time, experience increasing life satisfaction (Berggren et al. 2020).

However, the increase for the first generation will only add up to half of the difference between French and Nordic life satisfaction. In other words, these studies suggest a 50–50 result: Half of the life satisfaction of migrants from developed countries is shaped by their past, and the other half is shaped by the society they live in.

There is, nevertheless, very little research into the happiness and satisfaction of, for example, religious or ethnic minorities, not least because such research often requires specialized surveys – and conducting such surveys is extremely expensive. We therefore have a long way to go before happiness research fully understands where, why, and to what degree different minorities are affected by legislation, social norms, and society's tolerance. However, regardless of whether one measures the formal protection of minorities and how institutions ensure equal rights, or explores individual tolerance norms and respect for diversity, the Nordic countries rank among the freest societies in the world.

Chapter 8.

The many things that don't matter

As the previous chapters have demonstrated, there are a number of good reasons why some people and some entire societies are happier and more satisfied with their lives than other people and societies. Scientists always search for explanations, and those of us who deal in happiness research are no different: We try to understand why people and societies are happier, and therefore also, to some extent, what can be done to counteract unhappiness.

16.
In Bjørnskov, Dreher, & Fischer (2008), we looked at 70 different factors that other researchers had suggested might be important determinants of happiness. In several thousands of different tests, we found support for only one third of these factors, rejecting the other two thirds and causing much debate

One of the somewhat depressing findings in happiness studies is that most of the factors that researchers have thought might be (or ought to be) important turned out to be irrelevant.[16] But the mere fact that something is "irrelevant to happiness" does not make the finding itself any less important. When one searches for what *can* be done about a problem, it is equally important to know what *cannot* be done – which actions or policies are likely to be a waste of time and resources. The following therefore samples some of the many factors that are either known to be irrelevant or relate to happiness in a way that is more complex than most people seem to think. Some of these may be factors that many people believe are special to the Nordic countries and characterize their high levels of happiness.

Many things prove to be irrelevant to people's happiness and life satisfaction because we get used to them – we dynamically adapt our lives and our perceptions of what is "normal." For example, people buy large houses, believing that a new house will make them happier than the small apartment they had when they were younger. Sometimes a growing family simply requires a larger house, so a decision to move has more to do with necessity than increasing happiness levels, but in any case, most research shows that people rapidly adapt to a new house, whether they moved out of necessity or choice. The happiness gained by many objective improvements in our lives fades over time, and thus becomes surprisingly irrelevant in the long run.

Another reason why some things and circumstances may be irrelevant, even though many people strongly believe that they ought to affect happiness, is taste: The life your neighbor or cousin lives may simply not suit your tastes, your preferences, or your interests. These things are therefore *not* common to most people, although they may affect the happiness of people with specific preferences or personalities. A pertinent example is the belief that living in the countryside with plenty of room and a view of unspoiled natural surroundings makes people happier. It does undoubtedly make some people happier, but the effect is not shared by most people. The problem is that what some people perceive as a happy life in a serene place full of natural beauty – whether it has a view of the Catskill Mountains, a windswept Norwegian coastline, or a Swiss lake – will be perceived by others as a meaningless life in a tedious place with no hustle, bustle, or lively rapport with other people.

The Nordic welfare state

As noted before, one Nordic factor that most people know of around the world is the large, universal welfare state. The Scandinavian or, more broadly speaking, "Nordic" welfare model delivers a range of private goods and public services: Education, health services, social insurance, and basic unemployment benefits are "free," in the sense that they are funded by taxes that everyone pays. All Nordic states also redistribute substantial parts of total incomes through high and progressive taxes and large subsidies. For those who believe the Lerner argument – that money is more important to the happiness of poor people than that of richer people, and that redistribution in its different forms therefore causes *average* happiness to increase – it seems to follow directly and logically that a welfare model of the type and size found in the Nordics must create happiness.

The argument also rings true with many people because the two facts about these countries that are commonly known outside Scandinavia are (a) that they are among the happiest, and (b) that they have the most comprehensive welfare states in the world. The connection therefore seems clear: The welfare states must have created "Nordic happiness." However, as Ruut Veenhoven, one of the pioneers of happiness studies, documented in 2000, welfare states do *not* create happiness. Several studies have since shown that Veenhoven's finding was not a fluke, replicating his "non-finding." Experience shows the same basic pattern, as Denmark and Sweden both introduced significant reforms to their welfare states in the 1990s without their populations exhibiting any drop in life satisfaction. A number of recent studies even find that some types of welfare spending are detrimental to people's life satisfaction. A study from 2016 conducted by two German economists, Bodo Knoll and Hans Pitlik – which explores spending types and also the effects of spending on groups with low, middle, or high incomes – shows larger negative effects of welfare spending on high-income groups in society. The study shows that at best, increased welfare spending does not affect the satisfaction of poor people, while it harms that of relatively richer people. The question, therefore, is why welfare states do not affect the happiness of their citizens in either direction.

A first reason for the "non-effect" is that the welfare state's main role is resource redistribution, but as we saw in the discussion of income, a country's income distribution does not affect how happy its population is. In other words, 25 years of research gives us no reason to believe that income redistribution would affect a population's happiness or life satisfaction. It appears that as long as people perceive that the process that yields the income distribution is fair and transparent, whatever the distribution ends up looking like is fine. In addition, comprehensive or "extended" welfare states are always accompanied by high taxes, which, in the Nordic model, includes value-added taxes of 24–25%.

The second reason why comprehensive welfare systems do not affect happiness is adaptation: The welfare state mainly delivers services that citizens have not chosen themselves. Just as people rapidly change their expectations and their perceptions of what a "normal house" is after they move, they also change their expectations of what the public sector can and should deliver, relative to what is their own responsibility. Instead of making them happier, the welfare state simply means that people in the Nordic countries expect more extensive services from the state.

Third, the adaptation to living in a comprehensive welfare state also implies that most people learn specific ways of solving problems. In countries without a universal welfare model or with other types of welfare state, most people have individual health insurance, whereas people in the Nordics typically do not, since healthcare is provided by the state. Similarly, saving money for a child's college education or for a private pension tends to be a strategy used in countries outside the Nordics – which have welfare provisions for education and retirement. On the other hand, tax burdens outside the Nordic region are comparably lower. In other countries, civil society, including churches and philanthropic societies, alleviate similar problems, demonstrating the Nobel laureate Elinor Ostrom's insight that many problems in society have solutions grounded in the state, in markets, or in civil society. Indeed, the Nordic welfare states grew out of "benevolent societies" that the state gradually took over from the "hat ladies" – as the wealthy women who ran them were often called in Denmark, due to the large, fashionable hats of the late nineteenth century. As surprising as it may seem, many studies therefore find that high levels of inequality and social stratification, which could lead to limited access to health and education, and thus to lower happiness, are not clearly associated with how happy a population is.

Almost all Western countries address the same basic problems as the Nordic welfare states, but they do this in very diverse ways and with varying degrees of government involvement. The particular Nordic solution is only one of many feasible societal models, and it is a construction that can probably only work in the high-trust Nordics. I say this because it gives us the last piece of the apparent puzzle: It is practically impossible for a government to be able to implement a large, universal welfare state that offers uniform services to everyone if the population does not share the high-trust culture that characterizes the Nordics. Without high trust, too many people would try to cheat and evade the high taxes necessary to fund the "extended welfare state," the bureaucracy would become extremely expensive, and it is unlikely that many people would vote for the political parties that promote substantial redistribution of citizens' personal incomes to strangers. The "Nordic welfare model" and "Nordic happiness" appear to be closely linked to each other, but that is only because they share the same source: an uncommonly high level of social trust.

Is one gender happier than the other?

Another somewhat surprising non-finding is that in general, gender is irrelevant to happiness. Some studies find that women are happier than men, but other studies find the opposite, and many large-scale studies find no difference. There appear to be countries where men are happier than women, but there are also countries where women are happier than men, and what one finds in comparisons across countries depends on which exact countries the comparison covers. Theoretically the issue is also unclear, because one could argue that men might be happier than women because of gender discrimination, or point to the implicit repression women suffer when society takes traditional gender roles very seriously. However, one could equally argue that women might reasonably be happier than men, because traditionally men are the breadwinners of the family and often have harder and more dangerous jobs.

Gender differences in happiness are evident in the full seventh wave of the WVS, in which the two extremes are both found in the formerly communist countries: In Bulgaria, men are, on average, .29 points more satisfied than women, while in Albania, women are .52 points more satisfied than men. As illustrated in Figure 8.1, there are Western countries with and without a communist past between these extremes, and the only Nordic country that looks extreme is Finland, where women appear to be substantially happier than men. However, the reasons for these differences remain a mystery.

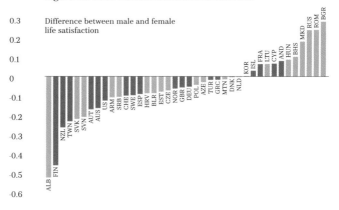

Figure 8.1 Male–female satisfaction differences

Education is not a source of happiness

Another potential surprise is that most studies find no direct effects of education on happiness or life satisfaction, although education is often thought of as a defining characteristic of modern society. Since Seymour Lipset's work in the 1950s, many social scientists, for example, see education as a necessary condition of a well-functioning democracy. A large body of literature on economics also identifies education as a source of innovation, competitiveness, and long-term growth. Even so, happiness is probably not one of its effects. Some studies even find that the most educated citizens in Western countries may actually be *less* satisfied with their lives than people with less education.

The problem of understanding the total effect of education is that people with more education also tend to earn higher incomes. Although the economic returns on education vary significantly from country to country, education nevertheless has an indirect effect on happiness and life satisfaction, either by making people richer or by reflecting special skills that make them richer. Generally, the higher income is going to result in higher happiness,

81

but wealthier people seem to be equally happier, whether their wealth is a result of their education or of something else – so education is just one way to become happier by becoming richer.

Other research has found that people with more education are more likely to find a steady, committed partner and thereby become happier, and they may also be more satisfied with their health. Conversely, several effects of more education may end up backfiring. The Italian sociologists Maria Laura and Gabriele Ruiu, for instance, have suggested in recent research that although highly educated people can typically find better jobs than less educated people, their level of education means that they also tend to have very high expectations and are more likely to experience frustration when their job and income expectations are disappointed. These additional effects may add up to a small positive or a small negative effect, but the only conclusion that can be made with confidence, based on the present literature, is that the additional effects of education are small and uncertain.

Is health important?

Another surprising finding in many happiness studies is that the effects of health are not obvious. Health is one of the most visible objective indicators of quality of life, and it remains an official goal of the United Nations. Health is also one of the aspects of life that is most often discussed in popular magazines, on TV, and in schools. However, just as is the case with evaluating the quality of a person's life, there are major differences between "objective health" and people's "subjective perception of health."

What appears to matter in studies where it is possible to separate these two views is respondents' own subjective perception – how satisfied they are with their health relative to their lifestyle (whether they smoke, drink, or eat too much, or exercise and keep in shape), and relative to whether they suffer from any disease or have a disability. In other words, people are happier when they have better health than would be expected, given their lifestyle. Perhaps paradoxically, people in objectively better health are therefore not necessarily happier, because they also have entirely rational, higher expectations regarding their health and their physical abilities.

Figure 8.2 illustrates how large the life satisfaction differences are with respect to *subjective* health. On the face of it, the differences in the figure suggest that subjective health may be *the* most important determinant of individual life satisfaction: The difference between the life satisfaction of people in "poor or very poor health" and those in "fair, good, or very good health" in the WVS is at least 1 point in all four regions. As such, it seems as if subjective health is even more important than finding the right life partner.

Nonetheless, extreme caution is advisable when studying and interpreting these differences. First, the simple fact that people are asked about their satisfaction with life, and soon after asked about their satisfaction with a specific facet of their life – their health – means that the answers to the two questions will tend to be similar for many people. Second, it is likely that the same factors, such as optimism and other personality factors, may affect the answers to questions about life satisfaction *and* health satisfaction. Such problems make the two measures deceptively similar and can easily cause one to overestimate the importance of health; hence the strong caveat.

It is certain, however, that subjective health is important, although it has a much smaller effect than indicated in Figure 8.2. Studies that follow the same people over several years can, for example, show what happens when people become more or less satisfied with their health. Overall, health is probably about as important as income, and far less important than enjoying good social relations or finding "the one."

Figure 8.2 Subjective health and happiness

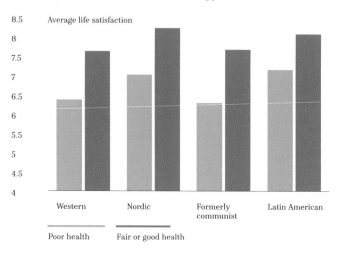

Does religion matter at all?

Some of the earliest happiness studies in the 1990s suggested that people who are more religious are also happier (Myers & Diener 1995). This claim made immediate, intuitive sense because religion is supposed to provide meaning to people's lives, to comfort them during hardship and heartbreak, and to promise a better life after this one. Early research also found that people who regularly attended religious services were happier. However, the role of religion is a question that more recent research has revisited – to find that the answer is not as simple as we first thought.

The Nordic countries are a case in point: The happiest region in the world also happens to be the least religious. Only one in six respondents state that religion is important in their everyday lives, and the most recent data from the European Social Survey suggest that some

84

3-4% of people in Denmark and Sweden regularly go to church. In comparison, 65% of all US citizens believe that religion is important in their lives, and more than half regularly go to church or attend some other religious service. This was the pattern that jarred many people in happiness research: How could the happiest countries in the world also be the least religious, when other studies showed that religion made people happier?

The answer to this conundrum is twofold. First, it appears that religion is important for happiness in relatively poor countries. When people live in absolute poverty, where there is a tangible risk that their children will not live to adulthood, and where poor institutions and unrest make life uncertain, religion does contribute to happiness with some form of comfort and meaning. In such countries, religious institutions are also regularly more trusted than government institutions, and they also provide food aid, other forms of support, and shelter for the poorest. In addition, most people in poor societies are clearly religious, which may make life difficult for non-believers, who are sometimes socially ostracized because they do not share the religious beliefs of their fellow citizens.

Conversely, religion seems to do relatively little for happiness levels in relatively rich countries.[17] As the sociologist Ronald Inglehart has shown, the problem with some of the early studies was that they used church attendance as their measure of how religious people are. However, he finds that church attendance in the US is related to "pro-sociality" more than to being religious. Inglehart finds that if a person attends a tennis club as often as other people attend church, then the avid tennis player becomes as happy as an avid church-goer. In the US, what was thought to be an effect of being religious turns out, mainly, to be an effect of having social relations and participating in voluntary associations or volunteer work. This is also visible in the data from the WVS, in which respon-

17.
In Bjørnskov & Tsai (2015), we explored the effects of various factors, finding a clear link between religion and life satisfaction in poor countries but not in rich ones. Further, Pöhls, Schlösser, & Fetchenhauer (2020) recently found that religiosity has little effect on life satisfaction in countries with largely irreligious populations

dents in Western countries, including those with a communist past, who state that they believe in God are only about 2% more satisfied than those who state that they do not. This difference is easily explained by the fact that "believers" also tend to be slightly more pro-social and active in associations than the irreligious. Conversely, Latin Americans who state that they believe in God are about 7% more satisfied than those who state that they do not.

A separate literature also indicates that religiosity can come with a side effect that directly reduces happiness: Strongly religious people tend to be less trusting than people who do not believe as strongly, or people who are atheists and agnostics. They trust other people who believe as strongly in the same type of religion they do, but they trust other people less and mainly interact socially with their own religious peer group. Both the lower levels of social trust and the constrained social relations typically lead to less happiness and life satisfaction. This means that there really is no paradox in the Nordic countries being happy, trusting, and irreligious all at the same time.

Chapter 9.

How old is Nordic happiness?

The widespread interest in the Nordic countries, and in their position among the happiest societies in the world because of their extremely high levels of social trust, is a recent phenomenon. It nevertheless begs the question of how old this Nordic exceptionalism is: Was the old Dano-Norwegian kingdom always happier than the rest of Europe, or is whatever makes today's Norwegians and Danes so happy due to social developments or policy changes in recent decades? Answering this question is complicated by the fact that almost all of our knowledge about happiness and satisfaction differences across the world comes from international surveys that often reach back in time only to the 1990s. An attempt to answer the question therefore requires us to explore not only the available survey evidence as far back as it reaches, but also the long-term stability of the factors that are known to contribute to Nordic happiness.

The first surveys conducted across multiple countries took place in 1973 and 1975; these were early waves of the EuroBarometer, a survey that covers all member states of what is now the European Union (EU). At the time, the union had nine member states, of which Denmark was clearly the happiest. In the latest surveys from 2019 and 2020, 45 years later, Denmark remains the happiest country in Europe, of the 35 that were surveyed. The stability of national happiness is illustrated in Figure 9.1, which plots the association between life satisfaction in 1973–1975 and in 2019–2020.

Figure 9.1 Life satisfaction 45 years apart

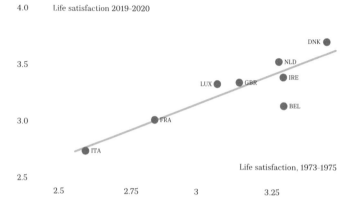

A similar pattern is seen, for example, in the WVS, which included four of the five Nordic countries in 1981, and in the GWP since 2006. In both cases, the Nordics remain among the most satisfied countries in the world, virtually always with Sweden as slightly less satisfied than the other four. To the extent it is possible to assess any "heritage of happiness" based on the available surveys, Nordic exceptionalism in terms of happiness seems to be at least forty years old, and remarkably stable.

What you learned from family and friends

In order to explain this stability and provide some indication of whether Nordic happiness is older than forty years, one must, instead, think about what might be the cause. One of the reasons behind the stability of happiness over time is that the sources of happiness are either learned or copied from our parents and grandparents. Many factors that shape our lives and our perceptions of our lives are characteristics that are perpetuated in our families. The American political scientist Eric Uslaner, for instance, has shown how modern-day Americans with Scandinavian grandparents are still more trusting than other Americans. Large parts of the high Nordic levels of social trust have thus survived for three generations in the US, and continue to make Scandinavian-Americans happier than people with other national origins.

Similarly, we tend to have risk attitudes that resemble those of our parents; we are about as optimistic and tolerant as they are; and we probably also copy or learn their freedom perceptions. A person's social trust and basic view of strangers are things that children typically copy from their parents within their first three or four years or life, while other attitudes such as tolerance norms are things that parents and other adults actively teach young family members.[18]

18.
The insight that social trust is perpetuated in the family is, in fact, older than the entire literature on the consequences of trust. It was first documented in Katz & Rotter (1968), now a classic in the literature

There is also reason to believe that a person's basic expectations of their life are learned within their family. If you grow up in a rich family, you are likely to grow up expecting that you too will have a large car and a nice apartment, and be able to afford interesting vacations. While there is relatively little research on family expectations, it is likely that children learn both good and bad attitudes from their parents. Children with Nordic parents are therefore mostly lucky in learning or copying high levels of social trust, strong tolerance norms, and very strong freedom perceptions. These family factors are likely to make them happier throughout their lives than people from different family backgrounds. They are also attitudes that children in the next generation will, most probably, learn from their parents, making happiness relatively stable over several generations.

The effect of stable institutions

Apart from what is perpetuated within the family, elements of a person's national environment can also remain stable over long periods of time, and a number of factors that are known to make people happy already existed in parts of the world a century ago. In particular, high levels of wealth, good judicial and bureaucratic institutions, and democratic traditions can be traced back a long way.

As far back as we can reasonably tell, Denmark and Norway have been among the richest countries in the world, with Sweden lagging slightly behind, but still setting the three Scandinavian countries apart. According to what is known as "the Madison database of historical income data," Denmark was the fourth-richest and Norway the fifth-richest of the 44 countries covered in 1850. By 1900, Norway was number six and Denmark number 10, while the two countries were back to being the second- and third-richest countries by 1935. Today, oil-rich Norway remains one of the richest countries in the world, while Denmark has dropped to number 30. Based on income differences alone, one would therefore expect the Nordics, or at least Denmark and Norway, to have been among the happiest countries relative to the rest of the world far back in history.

New research also suggests that the factors behind Nordic wealth in the second half of the nineteenth century are not just important in the Nordic countries, but also shape the situation in rich parts of the US today.[19] This research shows, in other words, that the particular Nordic cultural and institutional traits – especially those related to high levels of social trust and strong cooperative norms – that also make these societies happier today can

19.
Fulford, Petkov, & Schiantarelli (2020) show that, today, US counties with comparatively more families who can trace their origins back to relatively developed countries with strong cooperative cultural traits – not least the Nordics – are richer than other US counties

90

be traced back to the large wave of migration in the latter half of the nineteenth century.

Another indication of Nordic happiness existing far back in time comes from the historical fact that the Nordic region had high-quality judicial institutions. One source of this information is the *Varieties of Democracy* project, which assesses that among the 82 countries covered in 1850, Denmark had the best judicial institutions and the strongest rule of law, and that it ranked 73 out of 74 in terms of political corruption, just behind Switzerland and just ahead of Norway. Similarly, judging from the overall Rule of Law Index, Norway ranked fifth in the world, Sweden ranked thirteenth, and the much poorer Finland – then a province in the Russian empire – ranked eighteenth. The Nordic countries have a centuries-long history of untainted, well-functioning judicial and bureaucratic institutions that have contributed to a satisfied, fair society. It is therefore likely that the excellent institutions in these countries were already making their populations happier than most other places a century ago.

A further element that could have made the Nordic countries relatively happy a long time ago is admittedly speculative, but it is also suggestive: the particular characteristics of Nordic democracy. The political systems in the region are highly competitive, with between 8 and 10 parties represented in their parliaments and with frequent, large changes in the political landscapes and vote shares of the parties. This tradition also appears to be old.

Norway was the first country to take steps towards becoming a democracy. After the Napoleonic wars, when Norway briefly appeared to be on the verge of becoming an independent country (after 400 years in a "constitutional union" with Denmark), leading politicians wrote and implemented the democratic Eidsvoll Constitution. But instead of gaining independence, Norway was invaded by Sweden and forced to enter into a union with the Swedish king as its head of state. It nevertheless retained some of its own political institutions, including an elected parliament, and the Eidsvoll Constitution of 1814 would become the country's constitution when it finally gained full independence 91 years later. Very early on, Norway established and maintained a vibrant democratic tradition.

Similarly, when the first democratic elections were held in Denmark in 1834, the experts and the government were surprised to find that the population did not vote the way they had expected. Instead of voting for public figures of authority, such as priests, teachers, or wealthy people, they elected a diverse assembly of highly competent farmers and merchants, as well as members of the nobility. How independently minded voters were, and their willingness to act when given a choice, came as a genuine surprise to the political establishment. This trend would remain a political headache even after the adoption of a constitution 15 years later, introducing an elected national parliamentary chamber, and it would result in a long tradition of minority governments and broad political compromises.

Sweden has had a somewhat different political history from its close Scandinavian neighbors, while Finland – the first country in the world to grant women the right to vote (in local elections, in 1893) – has had quite a turbulent political history. Democratic political institutions appear to make people happier in most of the world, and given a definition of democracy as a situation in which the incumbent government is always in danger of being ousted, the Nordics seems to be one of the most democratic places in the world.

A final indication of how long the Nordics have excelled in happiness comes from travel guides from the nineteenth century, which became increasingly popular in the latter half of that century. While these guidebooks described beautiful sights, natural phenomena, and places worth visiting across the world, they were often critical of the norms and institutions of their destinations. Yet in the German and British classic series of guidebooks from the likes of Baedeker and Murray, there are no such warnings for the Scandinavian countries. Instead, the guides give the impression of peaceful, well-functioning societies where tourists need feel no more worried than they would at home in London or Berlin.

In summary, although no large, international surveys exist from before the mid-1970s – and given the impossibility of using time travel to procure historical data on life satisfaction – a number of indications suggest that the background for the Nordic countries' excellence in happiness existed as early as 100 years ago. The high levels of happiness and life satisfaction in these societies are not new, nor are they a result of recent policies or developments.

Chapter 10.

Conclusions

One of the important questions raised by modern happiness research and by the insights presented in this book is: Can other societies learn anything from the particularly happy Nordics? This is not only a big question – it is also difficult to answer, because how do entire societies learn? I cannot offer any definitive answers, but I do have some suggestions to consider.

It is not always the visible differences that are important. Many people, including the American talk show host Oprah Winfrey, who reported from Scandinavia, have argued that it must be the large welfare states that make the Nordic populations so happy or contented. The huge public sectors that take up more than half of people's incomes in Denmark and Sweden are plainly visible to outsiders, as are the substantial government redistribution and the relatively equal distributions of income. Other people have claimed that people in the Nordics are particularly modest and do not expect too much.

Research shows, however, that it is not the welfare state or the apparently modest expectations of life, and nor is it some magical balance between various facets of their lives that makes people in the Nordic countries so remarkably happy. Decades of research has shown how people get used to many things, including many types of material consumption, and perhaps specifically the types of consumption that we do not choose ourselves. Essentially, people very rapidly adapt to the welfare state and the particular ways in which the distinctly Nordic welfare model delivers services and insurance that other systems achieve in other ways. Research has also shown how our expectations are dynamic and – for the vast majority – adapt to what is realistic and seems achievable. It would be an odd country where the population continued to have low expectations of their lives while living in a democratic, rich, well-functioning society. When asked directly, people in the Nordic countries certainly do not report having low expectations of their lives, and in general they appear optimistic.

Similarly, it is not the case that the Nordics are richer than other Western societies like Canada, Germany, or the Netherlands. While Norway has grown rich due to its vast oil reserves in the North Sea, the other four countries rank between 25th and 38th on the list of the richest countries in the world. In other words, the Nordics are *not* happy because they are richer than other Western countries.[20] In addition, although it is well-known that the income differences between rich and poor are smaller in the Nordic countries than in most of the rest of the world, income equality is not a source of happiness. Comparing incomes alone, there is no reason why these countries ought to be happier than the rest of the Western world: Many countries are richer but have less satisfied citizens. However, research from the last twenty years clearly indicates that money matters, and that richer countries generally become happier over time.

Another factor that is central to happiness in the Nordic countries is the quality of their institutions. Judged by the *Varieties of Democracy* Rule of Law Index, Denmark had the world's strongest judicial institutions in 2019,

20.
Some even claim that individuals in the Nordics are less wealthy than in many other countries, due to high tax rates. According to the *CIA World Factbook*, private consumption accounts for 48% of all income in the Nordics, against 55% in other Western countries

with Norway at number 3; Sweden at number 4; Iceland at number 13; and Finland at number 15. Another indication of how different these countries are from the rest of the world is that they always rate at the top of Transparency International's annual anti-corruption list. Since the first version appeared in 1995, the organization has estimated that the least corrupt countries in the world are the Nordics, usually accompanied by Singapore and New Zealand.

Although the Nordics almost seem to have been "born" with good institutions, or at least to have maintained remarkably good institutions for more than a century, this circumstance is not set in stone. Several countries managed to establish (or reestablish) good institutions after communism collapsed in Central and Eastern Europe around 1990, and both Poland and Estonia have dealt with their corruption problems so successfully that they now rank among other Northern European countries. Similarly, Ghana in the mid-1980s and Singapore a decade earlier brought rampant corruption under control and now have much better and more politically independent judicial institutions than their neighbors.

Institutions can be improved when the political will exists and when citizens cooperate, and apart from the positive economic effects, better institutions are also likely to make people happier in the long run. There is no reason to believe that old institutions are better than young institutions at creating happiness and life satisfaction, as long as they are stable. The Nordics demonstrate to the rest of the world that it is possible to change happiness and life satisfaction in a country by strengthening its institutional framework.

However, some of the most important factors that make the Nordics the happiest region in the world are old. Vestiges of their high levels of social trust can also be found among the descendants of Scandinavian immigrants in the US who now populate Minnesota, parts of the

Dakotas, and parts of Oregon. No one knows how the high Nordic trust levels arose, or why they are so much higher than in the rest of the world. In 1782, the Scottish philosopher Adam Ferguson characterized such differences as "the result of human action, but not the execution of any human design." They are essentially institutions, norms, and habits that arose organically while people were minding their own lives.[21] The most famous of all these institutions is the Danish (and Norwegian) concept of *hygge* – an undefinable way of being together with other people without any agenda or expectations of anything other than confirming one's mutual support and sympathy – which can be traced far back in time. *Hygge* cannot easily be copied, but many foreigners who have moved to the Nordics recognize it when they meet it. An old adage says that the proof of the pudding is in the eating, and the same goes for *hygge*; it has to be experienced to be recognized.

When people are asked by the GWP whether they are satisfied with the freedom they have to choose what to do with their lives, an astounding 95% in the Nordics state that they are satisfied with their freedom. Similarly, when the WVS asked people about their sense of control over their lives, the average on a 10-point scale in both Western and formerly communist countries was 7.1, while the Nordics stuck out with an average of 7.7. Such freedom perceptions are also likely to have arisen spontaneously, such that the current inhabitants of the Nordic countries are simply lucky to have grown up with norms and personal beliefs that support a happy life.

Institutions that "emerge spontaneously," as Ferguson described, are difficult to copy exactly because they are not the result of any orderly, planned politics. However, this fact need not be worrying, as a number of habits and norms also change spontaneously with economic development. Although some of the changes happen across generations, when people become wealthier they gener-

21. Ferguson (1782) was a precursor to much recent thought on how civil society works in democratic societies. It remains an insightful and surprisingly modern book

ally also become more tolerant, demand more political influence, and accept fewer intrusions in their private lives. Some of the informal institutions that can vary a lot across countries are nevertheless a side effect of economic development, and they change as society develops and make the next generation happier.

Such side effects must be considered when discussing the value of economic development. When asking what other countries might learn from the Nordics, it is therefore important to remember that many historians have noted that in many ways the Nordics were more developed in the nineteenth century than their income levels would suggest. The Nordics were considered "impoverished sophisticates" – countries that were somehow ahead of the curve, with better-educated, more tolerant, and strongly individualist citizens well before other countries. Seen from this angle, learning from the Nordics may also be a matter of learning from Nordic history, and not simply from the modern societies in the region.

At the end of the day, the tale of Nordic excellence in happiness is a tale of trust, tolerance, good institutions, strong economic development for more than a century, and a resilient, lively culture of democracy. But perhaps it is also a tale of a somewhat unruly group of people who strongly believe that they have the freedom – and ought to exercise that freedom – to choose and lead the lives they think are best for them. One might even speculate that it is the Viking-style combination of high levels of prosocial trust and slightly disorderly, unregulated personal freedom that makes the difference.

Suggestions for further reading

Clark, A., Flèche, S., Layard, R., Powdthavee, N., & Ward, G.
(2018). *The Origins of Happiness: The Science of Well-Being over the Life Course.* Princeton University Press.

Frey, B. S. (2008). *Happiness: A Revolution in Economics.* MIT Press.

Gilbert, D. (2008). *Stumbling on Happiness.* Alfred Knopf.

Putnam, R. (1993). *Making Democracy Work. Civic Traditions in Modern Italy.* Princeton University Press.

World Happiness Report. (2021).

References

Alesina, A., DiTella, R., & MacCulloch, R. (2004). Happiness and Inequality: Are Europeans and Americans different? *Journal of Public Economics, 88,* 2009-2042.

Arpino, B. & de Valk, H. A. G. (2018). Comparing Life Satisfaction of Immigrants and Natives Across Europe: The Role of Social Contacts. *Social Indicators Research, 137,* 1163-1184.

Berg, M. C. & Veenhoven, R. (2010). Income Inequality and Happiness in 119 Nations: In Search for an Optimum that does not Appear to Exist. In B. Greve (Ed.), *Social Policy and Happiness in Europe,* 177-197. Edgar Elgar.

Berggren, N., Bergh, A., Bjørnskov, C., & Tanaka, S. (2020). Migrants and Life Satisfaction: The Role of the Country of Origin and the Country of Residence. *Kyklos, 73,* 436-463.

Berggren, N. & Bjørnskov, C. (2021). Institutions and Life Satisfaction. Forthcoming in Klaus F. Zimmermann (Ed.), *Handbook of Labor, Human Resources and Population Economics.* Springer

Berggren, N., Bjørnskov, C., & Nilsson, T. (2017). What Aspects of Society Matter for the Quality of Life of a Minority? Global Evidence from the New Gay Happiness Index. *Social Indicators Research, 132*, 1163-1192.

Bjørnskov, C. (2003). The Happy Few. Cross-Country Evidence on Social Capital and Life Satisfaction. *Kyklos, 56*, 3-16.

Bjørnskov, C., Dreher, A., & Fischer, J. A. V. (2008). Cross-Country Determinants of Life Satisfaction: Exploring Different Determinants across Groups in Society. *Social Choice and Welfare, 30*, 119-173.

Bjørnskov, C. & Foss, N. J. (2020). Wellbeing and Entrepreneurship: Using Establishment Size to Identify Treatment Effects and Transmission Mechanisms. *PLOS One, 15*, e0226008.

Bjørnskov, C. & Tsai, M.-C. (2015). How do Institutions Affect Happiness and Misery? A Tale of Two Tails. *Comparative Sociology, 14*, 353-385.

Brown, G. D. A. & Gathergood, J. (2020). Consumption changes, not income changes, predict changes in subjective well-being. *Social Psychology and Personality Science, 11*, 64-73.

Coleman, J. S. (1988). Social Capital in the Creation of Human Capital. *American Journal of Sociology, 94*, 95-210.

Easterlin, R. A. (1974). Does Economic Growth Improve the Human Lot? Some Empirical Evidence. In P. A. David and M. W. Reder (Eds.), *Nations and Households in Economic Growth: Essays in Honor of Moses Abramovitz*, 89-125. University of Michigan Press.

Ferguson, A. (1782). *An Essay on the History of Civil Society*. T. Cadell.

Festinger, L. (1954). A Theory of Social Comparison Processes. *Human Relations, 7*, 117-140.

Frey, B. S. (2008). *Happiness: A Revolution in Economics*. MIT Press.

Frey, B. S. & Stutzer, A. (2002). *Happiness and Economics: How the Economy and Institutions Affect Human Well-Being.* Princeton University Press.

Fulford, S. L., Petkov, I., & Schiantarelli, F. (2020). Does it Matter Where You Came From? Ancestry Composition and Economic Performance of US Counties, 1850–2010. *Journal of Economic Growth, 25,* 341–380.

Gilovich, T., Kumar, A., & Jampol, L. (2015). A Wonderful Life: Experiential Consumption and the Pursuit of Happiness. *Journal of Consumer Psychology, 25,* 152–165.

Hansen, T. (2012). Parenthood and Happiness: A Review of Folk Theories Versus Empirical Evidence. *Social Indicators Research, 108,* 1–36.

Hariri, J. G., Bjørnskov, C., & Justesen, M. K. (2016). Economic Shocks and Subjective Well-Being: Evidence from a Quasi-Experiment. *World Bank Economic Review, 30,* 55–77.

Helliwell, J. F. (2003). How's life? Combining individual and national variables to explain subjective well-being. *Economic Modelling, 20,* 331–360.

Jensen, M. F. (2013). *Korruption og Embedsetik: Danske embedsmænds Korruption i Perioden 1800–1866.* University of Southern Denmark Press.

Kahneman, D., Krueger, A. B., Schkade, D. A., Schwarz, N., & Stone, A. A. (2004). A Survey Method for Characterizing Daily Life Experience: The Day Reconstruction Method. *Science, 306,* 1776–1780.

Katz, H. A. & Rotter, J. B. (1968). Interpersonal Trust Scores of College Students and Their Parents. *Child Development, 40,* 657–661.

Kumara, A., Killingsworth, M. A., & Gilovich, T. (2020). Spending on Doing Promotes more Moment-to-Moment Happiness than Spending on Having. *Journal of Experimental Social Psychology, 88,* art. 103971.

Kuppens, P., Realo, A., & Diener, E. (2008). The Role of Positive and Negative Emotions in Life Satisfaction Judgment

Across Nations. *Journal of Personality and Social Psychology, 95,* 66–75.

Magee, C. S. P. & Doces, J. A. (2015). Reconsidering Regime Type and Growth: Lies, Dictatorships, and Statistics. *International Studies Quarterly, 59,* 223–237.

Myers, D. G. & Diener, E. (1995). Who is Happy? *Psychological Science, 6,* 10–19.

Odermatt, R. & Stutzer, A. (2019). (Mis-)Predicted Subjective Well-Being Following Life Events. *Journal of the European Economic Association, 17,* 245–283.

Ostrom, E. & Walker, J. (2003). *Trust and Reciprocity: Interdisciplinary Lessons for Experimental Research.* Russell Sage.

Powdthavee, N. (2008). Putting a Price Tag on Friends, Relatives, and Neighbours: Using Surveys of Life Satisfaction to Value Social Relationships. *Journal of Socio-Economics, 37,* 1459–1480.

Pöhls, K., Schlösser, T., & Fetchenhauer, D. (2020). Non-Religious Identities and Life Satisfaction: Questioning the Universality of a Linear Link between Religiosity and Well-Being. *Journal of Happiness Studies, 21,* 2327–2353.

Putnam, R. (1993). *Making Democracy Work. Civic Traditions in Modern Italy.* Princeton University Press.

Sanandaji, N. (2015). *Scandinavian Unexceptionalism: Culture, Markets and the Failure of Third-Way Socialism.* Institute of Economic Affairs.

Stadelmann-Steffen, I. & Vatter, A. (2012). Does Satisfaction with Democracy Really Increase Happiness? Direct Democracy and Individual Satisfaction in Switzerland. *Political Behavior, 34,* 535–599.

Stevenson, B. & Wolfers, J. (2008). Economic Growth and Subjective Well-Being: Reassessing the Easterlin Paradox. *Brookings Papers on Economic Activity, 39,* 1–102.

Uslaner, E. M. (2008). Where You Stand Depends upon Where Your Grandparents Sat: The Inheritability of Generalized Trust. *Public Opinion Quarterly, 72,* 725-740.

Veenhoven, R. (2000). Well-Being in the Welfare State: Level Not Higher, Distribution Not More Equitable. *Journal of Comparative Policy Analysis, 2,* 91-125.

Weber, M. (1904-5). Die Protestantische Ethik und der 'Geist' des Kapitlismus. *Archiv fur Sozialwissenschaft und Sozialpolitik, 20,* 1-54; and *21,* 1-110.